EC Public Procurement Law

EUROPEAN LAW SERIES

Series Editor:
PROFESSOR JOHN USHER

Published Titles

EC Public Procurement Law
CHRISTOPHER BOVIS

International Relations Law of the European Union
DOMINIC McGOLDRICK

EC Insurance Law
ROBERT MERKIN AND ANGUS RODGER

EC Consumer Law and Policy
STEPHEN WEATHERILL

EC Public Procurement Law

CHRISTOPHER BOVIS
Deputy Director, Institute of European Public Law,
University of Hull

LONGMAN
London and New York

Addison Wesley Longman
Edinburgh Gate
Harlow
Essex CM20 2JE
England

and Associated Companies throughout the world.
Published in the United States of America
by Addison Wesley Longman Inc., New York.

First published 1997

ISBN 0 582 29439 8 PPR

British Library Cataloguing-in-Publication Data

A catalogue record of this book is available from the British Library

Library of Congress Cataloging-in-Publication Data

A catalog entry for this title is available from the Library of Congress

Set by 7 in 10/12 Sabon
Printed in Great Britain in Henry Ling Ltd., at the Dorset Press, Dorchester, Dorset

Contents

Table of Cases

Case 13/61 *Kledingverkoopbedrijf de Geus en Uitdenbogerd v Robert Bosch GmbH* [1962] ECR 45 **89**

Case 26/62 *NV Algemene Transport-en Expeditie Onderneming Van Gend en Loos v Nederlandse Administratie der Belastigen* [1963] ECR 1 **78**

Case 57/65 *Alfons Luttucke GmbH v Haupzollampt Saarlouis* [1966] ECR 205 **27, 47, 78**

Case 28/67 *Firma Molkerei Zentrale Westfalen/Lippe GmbH v Haupzollampt Paderborn* [1968] ECR 143 **27, 78**

Case 13/68 *SpA Salgril v Italian Ministry of Foreign Trade* [1968] ECR 453 27

Case 167/73 *Commission v France* [1974] ECR 359 **79**

Case 2/74 *Reynes v Belgian State* [1974] ECR 631 **46**

Case 33/74 *Van Bisbergen v Bestuur van de Bedrijfsvereninging voor de Metaalinijverheid* [1974] ECR 1299 **46**

Case 36/74 *Walgrave and Koch v Association Union Cycliste International et al* (1974) ECR 1423 **32**

Case 43/75 *Drejenne v SABENA* (1976) ECR 473 **32**

Case 10/76, *Commission v Italy* [1976] ECR 1359 **79**

Case 133/80, *Commission v Italy* [1981] ECR 457 **80**

Case 76/81, *SA Transporoute et Travaux v Minister of Public Works* [1982] ECR 457 **91, 92, 95**

Case 283/81, *Srl CILFIT v Ministry of Health* [1982] ECR 3415 **90**

Case 249/81, *Commission v Ireland* [1982] ECR 4005 **93**

Case 247/83, *Commission v Italy* [1985] ECR 1077 **81**

Case 152/84 *Marshal v Southampton and South West Hampshire Area Health Authority* [1986] ECR 723 **33, 89**

Case 194/84 *P. Steinhauser v Ville de Biaritz*, before the Tribunal Administratif du Pau; judgment of 24 December 1987 before the District Court of Maastricht; and finally, an arbitration award of the Raad van Arbitrage of 31 March 1987. **90**

Case 199/85, *Commission v Italy* [1987] ECR 1039 **81**

Case 27/86, *Constructions et Enterprises Industrielles S.A (CEI) v Association Intercommunale pour les Autoroutes des Ardennes* **31, 92**

Case 28/86, *Ing.A. Bellini & Co. S.p.A. v Regie de Bâtiments* **31, 92, 94**

Case 29/86, *Ing.A. Bellini & Co. S.p.A. v Belgian State* [1987] ECR 3347 **31, 92**

Preface

I have always been fascinated by the European Communities and the new legal order established by European Community law. The creation, function and enhancement of a common market, envisaged by the founding fathers of the Treaty of Rome, is to be achieved through the progressive approximation of the economic policies of Member States. Such a market should have the characteristics of a genuinely open market, where effective and undistorted competition regulates its operation.

Public procurement has been considered as one of the most important non-tariff barriers for the completion of the common market, and its regulation has received priority by the European Union Institutions and the Member States. The liberalisation of public markets reflects the attempts of the European Union to enhance competitiveness in the public sector and industrial efficiency in order to achieve a uniform pattern of industrial policy.

The book aims to provide a comprehensive account of the subject, taking an interdisciplinary approach to the process of public sector integration in Europe. The objectives of the author are to familiarise students, academics, practitioners, executives and researchers with the mechanisms and practices of achieving the desirable effects of the integration of public markets in the European Union, the Member States and their main trading partners (USA and Japan); to assess the impact of legislation on public procurement in different legal and economic orders; to test the efficiency of the whole process of the liberalisation of the European Public Markets; and finally to evaluate any future developments of the European Union's policies with reference to public procurement.

It is hoped that the book will provide its readers with the broad framework of the function of public procurement and public purchasing in the common market and its Member States, and the legal and socio-economic parameters which determine this newly regulated field. It is also intended to facilitate an understanding and appreciation of the impact of the liberalisation of public markets on the whole process of European integration, as it places the regulation of public procurement within the framework of the four freedoms, as well as within European Union's key policies.

It would have been very difficult to finalise this book without the kind assistance of Brian Willan, Judith Bamber and Christopher Long, and the guidance of Professor John Usher, to whom I here record my great indebtedness. It is also with deep appreciation that I express my gratitude to officials of the European Commission and national administrations for their readiness to give me the benefit of their profound knowledge of the law and policy of public procurement. To Professor Patrick Birkinshaw and Dr Dimitri Mardas I am greatly indebted for the manner in which they kindly provided their expertise on legal and economic aspects of public procurement and public purchasing.

I am under the greatest debt of gratitude to Dr Christine Cnossen who did so much to further the completion of this work through her invaluable support and encouragement. Last, but not least, as a token of appreciation for everything he did for me, I dedicate this book to my father.

C. P. Bovis
March 1997

General Editor's Preface

The Longman European Law Series is the first comprehensive series of topic-based books on the EC Law aimed primarily at a student readership, though I have no doubt that they will also be found useful by academic colleagues and interested practitioners. It has become more and more difficult for a single course or a single book to deal comprehensively with all the major topics of Community law, and the intention of this series is to enable students and teachers to 'mix and match' topics which they find to be of interest; it may also be hoped that the publication of this series will encourage the study of areas of Community which have historically been neglected in degree courses. However, while the series may have a student readership in mind, the authors have been encouraged to take an academic and critical approach, placing each topic in its overall Community context, and also in its socio-economic and political context where relevant.

The law relating to public procurement is a matter which has recently gained prominence. This may in particular be ascribed to the fact that, as Christopher Bovis indicates, legislation in this area has been a priority for the European Community in the context of the completion of the internal market. The topic is of particular interest and importance as an illustration of the application of the rules of the EC single market in the public sector, and thereby justifies its inclusion in this series. Christopher Bovis also places the law relating to public procurement in the EC in the broader political and economic context, and I am most grateful to him for having made it accessible to a wide range of readers.

John A. Usher

Introduction

As the European Union moves deeper into its integration process and the establishment and functioning of a genuinely Common Market has to a considerable extent been materialized, the focus of attention of policy- and law-makers at both centralized and national levels has concentrated on eliminating non-tariff barriers that still exist and which pose obstacles to the operation of the Common Market.

The elimination of non-tariff barriers has been the target of European institutions over the past decade, particularly with reference to the completion of the Single Market in 1992. The European integration process, as an economic exercise which is based upon the concept of a customs union, could only succeed if non-tariff barriers were to be abolished. Such responsibility lies predominately in the hands of the member states, where through harmonization of their legislation and approximation of their administrative systems, genuinely competitive patterns of trade will bring about the desirable effects of economic growth and consequently an improvement of working and living conditions throughout the Common Market.

The European Commission's White Paper for the Completion of the Single Market[1] and the Single European Act which legally embodied it have set out the parameters for what has been described as the last chance of the European Community for successful integration. They identified public procurement as a potential and actual non-tariff barrier and immediate attention was given to the fact that protectionist public purchasing patterns

1. European Commission, *White Paper for the Completion of the Internal Market*, (COM) 85 310 fin., 1985.

had been distorting competition in the relevant markets of the member states. It should be mentioned here that basic legislation on the coordination of procedures for the award of public contracts has existed since the seventies, although its implementation, applicability and compliance have been characterized as, at best, ineffective. This hybrid set of rules on the regulation of public procurement during the early stages of the European Community was inappropriately transposed into national legal systems and, in fact, perpetuated existing protectionism and preferential public purchasing in the member states. The transposition of public procurement directives in member states' legal orders had been pursued by virtue of either national laws, or administrative practices, ministerial circulars and orders. The method of incorporation of public procurement directives into domestic legal orders had often relied on the preference that each member state had for public or private law regulation of public markets. The success of the incorporation of directives domestically depends mainly on the rights and obligations that are conferred on individuals. Implementation of directives through laws confers enforceable rights and duties upon individuals; administrative practices are not legally enforceable instruments and do not confer rights and obligations upon individuals of member states but they rather serve as legal guidelines, rather than as regulatory tools.

Before the completion of the Single Market, in 1992, France, Belgium, the United Kingdom, Spain, the Netherlands, Greece, Italy and Portugal had opted for statutory implementation of public procurement directives. On the other hand, Denmark, Ireland, Luxembourg and Germany relied on administrative practices in implementing them.[2] European institutions could not be attributed with the blame for inaction and indifference in observing the law and policy related to the award of public contracts in the member states and the relevant primary provisions of the Treaty of Rome that have an impact on public procurement, as a considerable number of cases under the compliance procedures of Article 169 of the Treaty of Rome have been launched against defaulting member states.

The Commission's White Paper for the Completion of the

2. For more details on the subject see the *14th FIDE Congress on Application in the Member States of the Directives on Public Procurement*, Madrid, 1990.

Single Market and the Single European Act formed the political and legal framework of the attempts of European institutions to tackle the issue of public procurement more effectively. New legislation was introduced and priority was given to the inclusion of the so far excluded public sectors (public utilities) into the regulatory regime of public procurement. The new set of European directives[3] have aimed at harmonization of national provisions for the award of supplies, works and services contracts in the public sector (comprising of central and local government and bodies governed by public law) and the utilities (entities operating in the water, energy, transport and telecommunications sectors). Emphasis was also placed on compliance of the above directives by member states and their contracting authorities and the availability of remedies to interested parties and aggrieved tenderers, so directives have been enacted which aim to ensure access to justice and sufficient compensation to tenderers that have suffered damages as a result of illegal acts of contracting authorities.[4]

The rationale behind the whole process of the integration of public markets of the member states has been the establishment of an effectively competitive regime, similar to that envisaged for the operation of private markets. In the *Suiker Unie* case (*Cooperative Vereniging 'Suiker Unie' UA v. Commission* [1975] ECR 1663), the European Court of Justice recognised the adverse effects of concerted practices in tendering procedures on competition within the common market. The *Suiker Unie* case appears to have opened the way for the application of competition law on public procurement in the Community. European institutions have intellectually supported such an attempt by reference to liberal economic theories, where enhanced competition in public markets could bring about beneficial effects for the supply side, by means of optimal allocation of resources within the European industries, rationalization of production and supply, promotion of mergers and acquisitions and elimination of sub-optimal firms, creation of globally competitive industries, effects which are deemed to yield

3. Public Supplies Contracts: EC Directive 88/295 (OJ 1988, L127,1), consolidated by Directive 93/36. OJ 1993, L199. Public Works Contracts: EC Directive 89/440 (OJ 1989 L210,1), consolidated by Directive 93/37, OJ 1993, L199. Utilities Sectors: EC Directive 90/531 (OJ 1990, L297), as amended by Directive 93/38, OJ 1993, L.199. Public Services Contracts: EC Directive 92/50, OJ 1992 L209.
4. EC Directives 89/665, OJ 1989 L395 and 92/13, OJ 1992 L76/7.

substantial purchasing savings to the public sector.[5] The way to create such a competitive regime in public markets has been seen by European institutions as the establishment of a legal framework that abolishes discrimination on grounds of nationality and eliminates preferential public procurement trends which favour 'national champions'. However, attempting to integrate public markets solely by reference to the regulation of the purchasing behaviour of the demand side (contracting authorities) leaves a large grey area of public procurement unaffected. Regulation of the supply side is equally important with reference to the attempts at regulation of public markets, but this has not been the subject of public procurement legislation. It seems that the assumptions of European institutions concentrate on the fact that by forcing contracting authorities throughout the Community into a common purchasing behaviour which is based on the principles of openness, transparency and non-discrimination, industrial restructuring (in the supply side) will follow, and therefore all the above-mentioned desirable effects concerning efficiency gains will occur.

These assumptions do not seem to take into account the inherent danger of market concentration as a result of such a stimulant to the demand side. Indeed, as sub-optimal firms are forced to leave the market and the volume of industrial concentration through mergers and acquisitions of less competitive firms grows, the danger of market oligopolisation becomes eminent. The applicability of competition law provisions of the Treaty (Articles 85 and 86) in controlling collusive tendering and anti-competitive behaviour of suppliers was also the subject of Commission Decision 92/204 (OJ 1992 L92/1). It could be argued that competition law and policy apply equally to private as well as public markets, but the explicit provisions of the directives on consortia participation in tendering procedures might limit the scope of Articles 85 and 86 in public procurement. Small and medium firms could find it difficult to penetrate particular product or geographical markets as a result of either collusive tendering of oligopolist suppliers, or inefficient own resources which could not be compared with those of large firms (volume production and

5. See the Cechinni Report, *1992 The European Challenge*, Aldershot: Wildwood House, 1988. Also, Commission of the European Communities, *The Cost of Non-Europe, Basic Findings*, Vol.5, Pt. A; The Cost of Non-Europe in Public Sector Procurement, Official Publications of the European Communities, Luxembourg, 1988.

economies of scale, financial and economic standing). Arguably, if the enhanced competitive regime in public markets results in industrial concentration which could bring about efficiency gains for public sector purchasing, then there is little scope for complaint about market inequalities concerning access and opportunities for small and medium firms. This, however, runs contrary to the declarations and undertakings by European institutions on the role of SMEs for the completion of the Common Market and its importance for regional and economic development, social cohesion and industrial adjustment. The fears regarding oligopolization of public markets and its subsequent effect of marginalization of SMEs have been confirmed.[6] Market access for SMEs in public procurement is limited and disproportionately low in relation to their numbers throughout the European Union.

In addition to the internal effects of the new regime, the integration of public markets has acquired an external dimension through the GATT Agreement on Government Procurement. Here, market access is guaranteed to firms established in signatories to the Agreement in an attempt to liberalize globally public procurement, although it was not until recently that contracting entities other than central authorities as well as construction procurement and procurement of services and telecommunications equipment were included in the Agreement, during the GATT Uruguay Round. In spite of the fact that the GATT Agreement on Government Procurement has been in existence since the Tokyo Round (1980), the tradability of public contracts *vis-à-vis* signatories to the Agreement has been rather limited. Import penetration for the public sector has been marginal and, again, large conglomerates appear to be the main beneficiaries of liberalization. European SMEs, particularly those in highly specialized industries, have been the target of US and Japanese takeovers, as the flow of direct investment within the European Union has increased over recent years. Interestingly enough, the vulnerability of SMEs, as a result of the global integration of public markets, follows similar patterns to those following internal public sector integration.

After all the attempts by European institutions to stimulate the demand side of public procurement in the member states, one

6. See Commission of the European Communities, *SME TASK FORCE: SMEs and Public Procurement*, Brussels, 1988; Commission of the European Communities, *Pan European Forum on Sub-Contracting in the Community*, Brussels, 1993.

could justifiably question the relatively slow progress and the underlying reasons behind such a recalcitrant rejection of the envisaged competitive regime in public markets. The answer seems pretty simple, although cynical in terms of reference to commitment to the European integration process and the completion and functioning of a genuinely common market in Europe. By perpetuating discriminatory and preferential public purchasing, member states respond to immediate needs relating to domestic and national priorities such as balance of payments, sustainability of strategic industries, employment and last but not least, national pride. This outcome, in terms of the envisaged integrated public markets throughout the European Union, represents a sub-optimal allocation of resources (human and capital) at the expense of the public sector, which pays more than it should for equivalent or even worse products or deliveries. The situation is tantamount to one of geographical market segmentation imposed by the demand side on the supply side, with a view to determining and controlling the latter as far as its activities *vis-à-vis* the public sector is concerned. It should be borne in mind that the supply side is unrestricted in servicing private markets in the respective member states.

This book aims to investigate the subject area from an interdisciplinary perspective. It endeavours to provide its audience with the broad framework of the function of public procurement and public purchasing in the Common Market and the member states, as well as the legal and socio-economic parameters which determine this newly regulated field. It also intends to enable its readers to understand and appreciate the impact of the liberalisation of public markets on the whole process of European integration, as it places and investigates the regulation of public procurement within the framework of the four freedoms, as well as within the European Union's key policies.

Chapter 1 attempts to define the parameters of the European integration process which are relevant to the public sector of the member states. The structure of the public sector in its purchasing dimension, as well as the magnitude of public procurement of contracting authorities in member states, reveal the real picture of the regime under examination. The constraints faced by European institutions and member states in their attempts to liberalize public procurement are also analysed.

In Chapter 2 we present and analyse the principles behind

public procurement legislation at European Union and national levels, the legal background of the regime, and its extraterritorial application and effects.

Chapter 3 provides a detailed analysis of the operation of public procurement legislation in the supplies, works, services and utilities sectors. Attention is paid to the importance of compliance and enforcement mechanisms of public procurement law at national and community levels.

In Chapter 4 the focus is narrowed on assessing the impact of public procurement legislation on the demand and the supply sides. The investigation covers the reaction of the contracting entities covered by the legal regime, the adaption of contracting entities to the principles of the directives, as well as the response of industry. A case study/codification, based on the litigation of the European Court of Justice (ECJ) and national courts on public procurement aspects, which classifies the main subject areas of the newly established regime that have attracted the attention and the rulings of the ECJ, completes this chapter.

Chapter 5 sets out to investigate the relationship between the regulation of public procurement with European Union policies, and in particular with social policy, regional development policy, defence and security policy and industrial policy. As part of the European Union's industrial policy, public procurement and its regulation represents a substantial policy-making armoury with respect to the stimulation of economic growth and industrial competitiveness in member states and in the Common Market, and has significant spillover effects on related policies which often bring into play questions of complementarity or incompatibility.

Finally, in the Concluding Remarks, we suggest some methods of assessing the impact of public procurement legislation on the process of the integration of public markets in the European Union.

CHAPTER ONE

The public sector and the European integration process

The Treaty of Rome and its amending Maastricht Treaty on European Union are based on the creation and functioning of a Common Market. The European integration process is primarily an economic one, with clear political spillover effects from its accomplishment. Whether the European Union will eventually become a full-fledged federal state is a topic that exceeds the scope and objectives of this book, although it should be pointed out that the economics of European integration present striking similarities to the economic function of federal systems. Not only free and unobstructed mobility of factors of production (labour and capital), but also the creation of a single currency and the adoption of a common economic and monetary policy are required by the Treaties for the completion of their aims. The European integration process is based upon a customs union, which will gradually become economic union, monetary union and finally political union. Clearly, the tool for such transformation is economic integration through the approximation of member states' economic policies and abolition of obstacles to trade. The level of success of economic integration in Europe will determine the level of success in political integration, as the ultimate objective stipulated in the Treaties.

There have been two strategic plans for the economic integration of the member states, which have been implemented by European institutions and transposed to law and policy by member states. The first is the abolition of all tariff or non-tariff obstacles to trade amongst member states. The second plan is the establishment of an effective, workable and undistorted regime of competition within the Common Market, where abuse of market dominance and cartelization could have serious economic implications in its functioning. The first plan appears to have a static effect aimed at abolishing all administrative and legal obstacles to free trade and has had as its focal point member states and their national administrations, whereas the second plan has been addressed at industry level and has a more ongoing and dynamic effect.

All tariff barriers were abolished by the end of the first transitional period (31 December 1969), so customs duties, quotas and other forms of quantitative restrictions could no longer hinder the free flow of trade between Member States. Non-tariff protection, however, has proved more difficult to eliminate, as it involves long-established market practices and patterns that could not change overnight. In the list of non-tariff barriers we include public monopolies, fiscal factors such as indirect taxation, state aids, technical standards and, last but not least, public procurement. The above could distort the operation of the Common Market and its fundamental freedoms by means other than tariffs. Trade patterns are hindered as a result of the existence of non-tariff barriers, and all the attention has been directed on how to eliminate them.

The European Commission's White Paper for the Completion of the Single Market[1] identified existing non-tariff protection and provided the framework for specific legislative measures in order to address the issue at national level. A set of directives was deemed necessary for the completion of the Single Market by the end of 1992, and the timetable was set out in the Single European Act, which in fact amended the Treaty of Rome by introducing, *inter alia*, the concept of the Single Market. The Single Market, in quantifiable terms, could be considered as something less then the Common Market, but perhaps the first and most important part of the latter. As mentioned earlier, public procurement was identified as an actual non-tariff barrier and action was scheduled to address the issue. The European Commission based its strategy on two notable studies,[2] where empirical proof of the distorted market

1. European Commission, *White Paper for the Completion of the Internal Market*, (COM) 85 310 fin., 1985.
2. See Commission of the European Communities, *The Cost of Non-Europe, Basic Findings*, Vol. 5, Pt.A; The Cost of Non-Europe in Public Sector Procurement, Official Publications of the European Communities, Luxembourg, 1988. Also the Cechinni Report, *1992 The European Challenge*, Aldershot: Wildwood House, 1988.

situation in the public sector was highlighted and the benefits of the regulation of public procurement were emphasized.

The volume and structure of public procurement in the member states

The stakes behind the regulation of public procurement and the integration of public markets in the European Union are so high that the whole issue became a priority overnight. The magnitude of public procurement in the Europe of 12 has been estimated at ECU 560 bn, approximately 15 per cent of the Community's GDP. These figures were based on 1988 prices. The reader should not be surprised if the figures approach ECU 750 bn at 1996 prices, with the latest enlargement of the EU taken into account. In real terms, public procurement represents a significant amount of the member states' GDP, a fact that has been seen as very important by European institutions. Given the level of infrastructure and the amount spent on it every financial year by contracting authorities of the member states, the public sector has acquired a significant dimension within the European integration process, and the need to regulate it with a view to eliminating market distortions has become urgent.

The reader is provided with an indication of the public procurement volume and structure of twelve of the present member states for which data are available. As far as the purchasing structure is concerned, two main categories of systems can be distinguished: the first relies on a centralized control of the procurement requirements of the contracting authorities, whereas the second allows for more autonomy at regional level. Of course, there are cases where a combination of centralized and decentralized procurement practices exist, as a result of long-standing administrative structures which predate European legislation. One could not easily criticize the operation of a domestic purchasing system by reference to the centralized or decentralized nature of the national administration. Member states have their own administrative/public systems, which to a certain degree give priority to centrifugal or centripetal structures. Public procurement arrangements cannot escape such long and well-established patterns, and there is no substantial evidence that change in the structural nature of national administrations would benefit the state and its contracting authorities when purchasing supplies, works or services. Bearing in mind that the principle of subsidiarity is now well founded by virtue of the Maastricht Treaty on European Union, it would be a *contradictio in terminis* to deny peripheral responsibility throughout the common market, as far as procurement is concerned.

The only structural change in the domestic public systems that has been suggested by European institutions and which is not related to the division of powers between central and local goverenment, is the privatization of state-controlled enterprises. The reader will recall that public monopolies, often operating in the utilities sectors, have been considered as actual and potential non-tariff barriers. Privatization will bring about changes in the ownership of such enterprises and raise capital for the government, but is not expected to result in significant changes in structural purchasing patterns. Utilities, whether state-controlled or privatized, are in any case subject to the public procurement directives.

The figures provided in Table 1 show national public procurement above certain thresholds which trigger the application of the relevant directives (dimensional public procurement). The volume of public procurement contracts which are not covered by the directives is much higher and more difficult to monitor with accuracy. Data for the public sector purchasing of the new member states (Sweden, Finland and Austria) were not available at the time of writing.

Table 1 ***Public procurement markets in European member states, 1994***

Member state	Total public procurement (EU m.)	Supplies and services procurement (ECU m.)	Construction procurement (ECU m.)
United Kingdom	65,206	51,904	13,302
Belgium	26,938	11,557	9,326
Denmark	21,482	9,216	6,493
Germany	176,927	51,310	24,891
Italy	142,456	31,079	19,359
Luxembourg	1,253	538	124
Portugal	7,042	1,536	896
Spain	52,866	11,534	9,423

Table 1 *(cont)*

Member state	Total public procurement (ECU m.)	Supplies and services procurement (ECU m.)	Construction procurement (ECU m.)
Ireland	5,936	3,150	958
France	69,897	45,533	24,464
The Netherlands	25,412	8,200	7,171
Greece	6,531	3,830	1,027

Sources: Commission of the European Communities, *The Cost of Non-Europe in Public Sector Procurement*, 1990; National Westminster Bank, *Economic and Financial Outlook*, 1994; OECD, *Economic Outlook*, December 1994.

The figures in Table 1 shed light on the cumulative magnitude of public sector procurement in the European Union and reveal the relative importance in terms of volume of procurement of supplies and services for member States. Public construction work follows a similar pattern in all European member states in relation to the procurement of supplies and services. An analysis of the public sector purchasing structure in the member states is provided below.

United Kingdom

The structure of British public procurement can be classified into five major types of contracting entities. These include central government, with its various departments and agencies, including the Ministry of Defence (MoD) in its capacity as a procurer of supplies for non-military purposes; local authorities, subdivided into county, district and borough councils; the National Health Service (NHS); public utilities operating in the water, telecommunications, energy and transport sectors, the majority of which have been privatized or are in the process of privatization; and finally other types of public entities covered by public procurement legislation, such as quangos (quasi-autonomous non-governmental organizations), universities and other higher education institutions. With reference to the purchasing power of public authorities, central government is responsible for 27 per cent of the total public procurement, local authorities (including the NHS) for 25 per cent and the MoD for 26 per cent. Public utilities account for 15 per cent, and finally quangos and other non-governmental bodies for 7 per cent of total public procurement in the United Kingdom.

France

The structure of French public purchasing can be classified into three major types of contracting entities. These include (i) central government with its various departments and agencies, including the ministry of defence in its purchasing capacity for civilian purposes, (ii) local authorities and (iii) public corporations (utilities) operating in the water, telecommunications, energy and transport sectors. French public procurement is a rather complex business. The existing domestic procurement practices survived most of the changes brought about by European directives and provide a very fragmented picture of the French public sector. The latter could be characterized as being highly decentralized in principle, with complicated administrative structures. The only centralized feature of French public procurement is the Union des Groupement d'Achats Publics, which acts as a central procurement agency for public purchasing. Although in the past it was vested with significant powers and tasks, it is now used by few ministries for the purchases of specific products, most government departments having their own procurement systems. Local and regional authorities as well as communes are also vested with procurement powers. Utilities are in the form of public corporations and have monopoly status in both production and distribution, as well as in the form of concessions. The highly fragmented and decentralized French public sector presents difficulties in respect of its monitoring. Central government and local authorities have more or less equal shares in public procurement, accounting for 28 per cent and 25 per cent respectively. Public utilities are responsible for the remaining 47 per cent of total public procurement.

Netherlands

Dutch public purchasing can be classified as decentralized. The body which acts as the intermediary between suppliers and public entities is the Rijkinskoopbureau. The Rijkinskoopbureau was subject to privatization and as a consequence, it currently charges public entities for the procurement services it provides. This has resulted in a major restructuring of Dutch public procurement and many of the central government departments now undertake their own public procurement. Decentralization occurs in the utilities as well. For electricity, there are provincial and municipal authorities. For oil and gas, the main entities are Nederlandse Gasunie and Petroland BV, besides a large number of distribution companies. For water, there are numerous local authorities (Wanderleidings Wet). Transport is in the hands of Nederlandse Spoorwegen NV for railways and KLM for air services, while post and telecommunications are the responsibility of Staatsbedrijfer der Ponteijen, Telegraphie en Telefonie. Central government controls a modest proportion of public procurement (15 per cent), while local authorities and public utilities are accountable for 57.5 per cent and 27.5 per cent respectively of total public procurement.

Ireland

The structure of Irish public purchasing can be classified as centralized. The Government Supplies Agency is the official body responsible for Irish public procurement. In addition, however, most government departments maintain their own purchasing sections. Local authorities comprise county councils, county borough corporations, borough corporations and urban district councils. The Irish Republic's utilities sector includes six major purchasing authorities. Gais Eireann is responsible for the distribution of natural gas, whilst the Electricity Supply Board generates and distributes electricity. Purchasing for the water sector is conducted at the local level. In the travel and transportation sectors, Coras Iompair Eireann is responsible for bus (Irish Bus, Dublin Bus) and train (Iarnrod Eireann) operations. Aer Lingus is the wholly state-owned national airline, while the three major airports are managed by Aer Rianta. Postal services are provided by An Post and Telecom Eireann is responsible for telecommunications services. Central government and public utilities have more or less equal shares in public purchasing, with 25 per cent and 27.5 per cent respectively, while local authorities (including health boards) account for 47.5 per cent of the total public procurement.

Denmark

The structure of Danish public purchasing can be classified as decentralized. Central and local government are responsible for their own procurement, accounting for 28.7 per cent and 36.9 per cent respectively as a proportion of total public procurement. Local authorities own most of the energy companies in the electricity and gas sectors; there are several water authorities which are responsible for their own procurement requirements. Public transport and telecommunications are under state control, through the Danske Statsbauer and the Post os Telegrafvaesenet respectively, although lately some telecommunication services, including mobile telephony, have been privatized. Public utilities procurement accounts for 34.4 per cent of the total public purchasing in Denmark.

Germany

German public procurement has been highly decentralised. The federal governement has sixteen ministries responsible for their own procurement. Federal states (*Länder*) posess autonomy in their procurement, whereas the same occurs for the police and educational institutions. Electricity supply is provided by the Deutsche Verbundgesellschaft and distributed via distribution companies often owned by the *Länder*. Local authorities also own gas production and distribution companies. Water supply is undertaken at *Länder* level. Rail transport is controlled through the Deutsche Bundesbahn. Air transport is state-controlled and the operation of Germany's civil airports is the responsibility of companies owned by the *Länder*. Telecommunications and postal services are the respnsibility of the Deutsche Bundesposte. The central administration has a 13.8 per cent share of annual public procurement in Germany, while local authorities account for 39.5 per cent. Public utilities are responsible for 46.7 per cent of total public procurement in Germany.

Italy

The structure of Italian public purchasing is *sui generis*. It can be described as a mixture of centralized and decentralized procurement control. At central level, the Proveditorato Generale dello Stato is responsible for procurement on behalf of government departments, although all major ministries additionally have their own procurement responsibilities, which can be delegated at regional and local levels. At regional level, the Agenzia per la Promozione dello Sviluppo del Mezzogiorno is the body responsible for procurement on behalf of regional and local authorities, particularly those in the southern part of Italy. Energy is generated by the state-controlled company Ente Nationale Energia Elettrica (ENEL) and supplied by regional companies owned by municipalities. Water supplies are the responsibility of local authorities, which undertake the relevant procurement. Air and rail transport are state-controlled by Alitalia and Aero Trasporti and Ferrovie dello Stato respectively. Telecommunications and postal services are also in public hands through the Amministrazione delle Poste e Telecomunicazioni and the Societa Italiana per l'Esercizio delle Telecommunicazioni. Central government is responsible for 16.8 per cent of total public procurement, whereas local authorities are responsible for 24.8 per cent. Additionally, 27.9 per cent is spent on social security and health, mainly through *enti pubblici*, a category of contracting authorities which usually are independent of central or local administration control. Utilities account for 30.4 per cent of Italian public purchasing volume.

Spain

Spanish public purchasing has centralized characteristics. Four major ministries are responsible for the bulk of procurement at central and regional level. Public utilities are state-controlled. ENHER and ENDESA are the state electricity companies, ENGAS the gas distributor. Water supplies are managed through ten management authorities. Rail and air transport are controlled by National de los Ferrocarriles Españoles and Iberia respectively. Postal and teleccommunications services are controlled by PTT and Companie Telephonica Nacional de España respectively. Public procurement by central government and local authorities accounts for 13.9 per cent and 18.1 per cent respectively of the total public procurement. An additional 10.9 per cent is spent on social security, mainly through central government. Public utilities are responsible for 56.9 per cent of the public procurement volume in Spain.

Luxembourg

Luxembourg has a mixed centralized and decentralized procurement system. Each central government ministry undertakes its own purchasing. Central coordination occurs through the Service Central des Imprimes et des Foumitures de Bureau de l'Etat which purchases all office supplies, the Administration des Bâtiments Publics, which procures all furniture and fuel, the Centre Informatique de l'Etat, which purchases all data processing equipment, and the Ministère des Travaux Publics, which is responsible for all civil engineering and building work. Only ten administrative districts of the 130 in the Grand Duchy have powers to place public contracts, although the smaller districts sometimes establish purchasing consortia for particular procurement projects. The Société Electrique de l'Our SA imports supplies mainly from Belgium and Germany. For oil and gas, the principal supplier is the Société de Transport de Gaz (SOTEC) which imports, transports and delivers gas. The water industry is controlled by ten inter-municipal syndicates, with extensive procurement powers. The railways are controlled by the Société Nationale des Chemins de Fer Luxembourgeois (SNCL), which is publicly owned. The Administration des Postes et Telecommunications controls all postal and telecommunication services. Central government has a 38.8 per cent share of the total public procurement in Luxembourg, whereas local authorities are responsible for 24.5 per cent. Public utilities account for 36.7 per cent of the total public procurement volume.

Portugal

The Portuguese system appears rather centralized. Public purchasing lies in the hands of five major ministries, which are responsible for central government procurement. The public monopoly Electricidade de Portugal controls the electricity sector; there is no state involvement in the oil and gas industry at all. The Correois e Telecommunicacoes de Portugal EP provides most of the postal and telecommunication services, and Telefones de Lisboa e Porto EP handles the telephone services in Lisbon and Oporto. Air services are state-controlled by Aeroportos e Navegação (ANA), while rail services are operated by Caminhos de Ferro Portugueses EP. Water supplies and services are purchased by the regional municipal authorities. Central government accounts for 29.4 per cent of the total public procurement, whilst local authorities have a modest 11.4 per cent share. Public utilities are responsible for 57.1 per cent of the public procurement volume in Portugal.

Greece

The structure of the Greek public procurement sector could be classified as centralized. Central government purchasing is pursued throught various ministries. They pursue public procurement by requests which are sent to one of four public purchasing directorates at the Ministry of Commerce. Greek public procurement is relatively transparent and competitive since it is mainly based on open tenders. In the utilities sector, most of the industries are publicly owned. For coal mining and for electricity generation and distribution the relevant authority is the Public Power Corporation. For oil and gas supply, the purchasing authority is the Public Petroleum Corporation (DEP); and, for distribution the Athens Municipal Gas Enterprise (DEFA) is responsible. The Athens Water and Sewage Corporation (EYDAP), the Thessaloniki Water Authority and the Municipality of Patras are the major purchasers in the sewerage sector. Railways are state-owned through the Organismos Sidirodomon Ellados (OSE). Air services are state-owned and controlled by the Ministry of Transport and Communications. Postal and telecommunications services are provided by the state-owned Hellenic Post (ELTA) and the Hellenic Telecommunications Organization (OTE), respectively. Central government controls 25 per cent of public purchasing, whereas local authorities and public utilities are accountable for 38 per cent and 37 per cent respectively of the total public procurement.

Belgium

The Belgian purchasing system is highly decentralized, although there is a significant degree of publicly owned and controlled procurement in Belgium, through central ministries. Over half of public procurement is undertaken by local government. There is a high degree of purchasing autonomy, even down to the level of the 589 local communes. Electricity supply is mainly privately generated, but the distribution network is shared between the public and private sectors. Oil and gas are primarily publicly controlled, by Detrofina and Distrigaz. The Société Nationale de Distribution d'Eau (SNDE) purchases goods and services for the water industry. Sewage and waste water treatment is provided by eight inter-communal companies. Rail transport is provided by the Société National de Chemin de Fer (SNCB), which procures all its own services and products. The federal government owns air transport services through the Régie des Voies Aériennes (RVA); postal and telecommunication services are state controlled through through the Régie des Poste and the Régie des Telegraphes et des Telephones, respectively. Central government public purchasing accounts for 19.7 per cent of the total public procurement in Belgium. Local authorities are responsible for 57.5 per cent and public utilities for 22.8 per cent of the public procurement volume.

Constraints in integrating the public sector of the European Union

The European Commission claimed that the regulation of public procurement throughout its member states and the resulting elimination of non-tariff barriers arising from discriminatory and preferential purchasing patterns could bring about substantial savings of ECU 20 bn, or 0.5 per cent of GDP to the public sector.[3] Combating discrimination on grounds of nationality in public procurement and eliminating domestic preferential purchasing schemes could result in efficiency gains at European and national levels through three major effects which would influence the supply side. These include a trade effect, a competition effect and a restructuring effect. The trade effect is associated with the actual and potential savings that the public sector will be able to achieve through lower purchasing costs. This effect appears to have a static dimension. On the other hand, the competition effect relates to the changes of price behaviour of national firms which have been protected from competition by means of discriminatory procurement practices. Finally, the third effect reflects the restructuring dimension in the supply side as a result of increased

3. Commission of the European Communities, *The Cost of Non-Europe, Basic Findings*, Vol. 5, Pt.A; The Cost of Non-Europe in Public Sector Procurement, Official Publications of the European Communities, Luxembourg, 1988.

competition. The restructuring effect is a dynamic one and refers to the long-term industrial and sectoral adjustment of industries that supply the public sector.

The above scenario seems to overlook the socio-economic and to some extent legal parameters of the integration of public markets in the European Union. The Commission's idea on the liberalization of public procurement and the beneficial effects that will allegedly follow as a result of the stimulant reaction of the supply side does not fully take into account contraints which may hinder the delivery of the envisaged results under such a scenario. Potential and actual problems focus on three main areas: public monopolies and the process of their privatization in the member states, harmonization of standards and specifications, and finally inherent constraints of the legislation.

Public monopolies, often operating in the utilities sector (energy, transport, water, telecommunications), have been the target of a sweeping process of transformation to competitive enterprises. These legal or delegated monopolies have been assigned with the exclusive exploitation of the relevant service in their respective member states, and very often possess a monopsony position. State-controlled enterprises follow a somewhat different management pattern than private ones in their market activities. Profit maximization is not their main objective, and decision-making responds not only to market forces but also, in large part, to political pressure. Understandably, their purchasing behaviour reflects, to a large extent, current trends of industrial policy of the government in power. It has become apparent that public monopolies in the utilities sector have sustained industries in member states through exclusive or preferential procurement. Such purchasing behaviour could not easily withstand the competitive forces to which private firms are exposed. Sustainability of 'national champions', or in other terms, strategically important enterprises, could only be achieved through discriminatory purchasing patterns in member states. Privatization of the public monopolies which absorb, to a large extent, the output of such industries will most probably result in a discontinuation of such patterns and may lead to industrial policy imbalances, as it will be difficult for firms to secure new markets to replace their traditional long dependency on public monopolies. Imbalances in social policy will also occur, as a result of the restructuring of the public monopoly and dependent industries.

Public monopolies in the European Union, which are mainly utilities, are responsible for a substantial magnitude of procurement, in terms of both volume and price. This is due to the expensive nature of the utility infrastructures and the high technology products that are necessary to procure in order to deliver the desired services to the public. Given the fact that most suppliers to public utilities are dependent on them and that, even when some degree of privatization has been achieved, often the *de facto* control of the utilities remains vested in the state, the first constraint on liberalizing public procurement in the European Union is apparent. Utilities, in the form of public monopolies or private enterprises, appear prone to perpetuating long-standing over-dependency purchasing patterns with certain domestic suppliers. Reflecting the above observations, the reader should bear in mind that until 1991, utilities were not covered by European legislation on procurement. The delay in the extension of this regulation can be attributed to the resistance from member states in privatizing their monopolies and the uncertainty of the legal regime that would follow their privatisation.

National technical standards for industrial products specification and their harmonization were considered priority areas for the Single Market programme. The European Commission's White Paper for the Completion of the Single Market stipulated that a number of directives should be adopted and implemented with a view to eliminating discrimination based on national standards. The rules on technical standards and specifications have been brought in line with the new policy, which is based on the mutual recognition of national requirements, where the objectives of national legislation are essentially equivalent, and on the process of legislative harmonization of technical standards through non-governmental standardization organizations (CEPT, CEN, CENELEC).[4] However, the persistence of contracting authorities in specifying their procurement requirements by reference to national standards poses obstacles to public sector procurement integration.[5] The most notable examples of

4. Article 7 of Directive 88/295. See the White Paper on Completing the Internal Market, paras. 61–79; also Council Resolution of 7 May 1985, OJ 1985, C136, on a new approach in the field of technical harmonization and standards.

5. See the documents of the Advisory Committee for the Opening up of Public Procurement, *Policy Guidelines on the Obligation to Refer to European Standards*, CCO/91/67 fin.; Advisory Committee for the Opening up of Public Procurement, *Standards for Procurement*, CCO/92/02.

circumvention of the policy on standards and specifications include the familiarity of national suppliers with technical data existing in a member state, over-specification by contracting authorities in order to exclude potential bidders, and finally favouritism and discrimination by contracting authorities by making available technical standards and specifications to certain suppliers only.

Inherent shortcomings in the legislation also pose obstacles to the integration of the public sector in Europe. The directives allow the division of public contracts into smaller lots without any justification from contracting authorities. This can facilitate intentional contravention of the directives, which do not apply below certain size thresholds. In addition, certain types of award procedures (particularly negotiated and restricted) and of award criteria (particularly the most economically advantageous offer) are prone to abuse by contracting authorities in order to favour certain suppliers or contractors.

As a concluding remark in this chapter, protectionism in public procurement and continuing resistance to public sector integration reflect the concerns of the member states to maintain employment and social equity, together with a broader goal of promoting greater economic efficiency and industrial adjustment within their borders. Balance of payments considerations, lower transport and trading cost, quicker delivery and more efficient after-sales service can also represent good reasons for making purchases from 'national champions'. The integration of the public sector in the European Union through the liberalization of public purchasing should achieve a fine balance between efficiency gains and the implementation of domestic policies which are closely related to public procurement.

CHAPTER TWO

The legal background of public procurement in the European Union

The legislative framework of public procurement

The Treaty of Rome and its amending Maastricht Treaty on European Union do not contain explicit provisions on public procurement. However, there is no doubt that provisions on non-discrimination (Article 7), on the prohibition to barriers to intra-Community trade (Article 30 *et seq.*), on the freedom to provide services (Articles 52, 53), on the right of establishment (Articles 59, 60), and on public undertakings and undertakings to which member states grant special or exclusive rights and state monopolies providing services of general economic interest (Article 90), can be applied in order to regulate government purchasing and combat discriminatory procurement practices in the member states. Nevertheless, the diversity of public law systems in the European Union and the peculiarities in existing domestic public procurement rules would have rendered ineffective the regulation of public markets, if recourse to primary Community legislation alone was sought.

In order to regulate public markets, Community institutions have opted for directives, since they are legal instruments which take into account existing national sensibilities and particularitics in member states' legal systems. European directives are flexible legal instruments, not only because they leave the choice of the form and methods of their implementation in the hands of member states, but also because they provide for a specified period within which the latter must implement their provisions. A directive has binding force with respect to the result to be achieved within each member state to which it is addressed. The fact that the form and methods of implementation are left to the discretion of the addressee member states reveals the unique character of such legal instruments, for which there is no parallel in national or international law.

Although directives generally aim at the harmonization of national laws of member states, the directives on public procurement mention as their objective the coordination of national procedures for the award of public contracts. Using the term 'harmonization of laws', the EEC Treaty envisages the gradual approximation of existing national legal provisions. These provisions are legally enforceable in member states: legal orders conferring rights and duties upon individuals. On the other hand, coordination as a term used by Community law appears relevant with respect to national policies. National policies are not always incorporated in legal instruments, but they may constitute governmental approaches towards the achievement of an aim. The fact that a state may prefer to regulate a sector through administrative practices and not statutorily might reflect the complexity of the sector in question. Administrative practices are not legally enforceable instruments and do not confer rights and obligations upon individuals of member states. They serve as legal guidelines, rather than as regulatory tools. Thus, coordination of national policies is a more relaxed procedure than harmonization of laws. The latter is a requirement for uniformity among the member states' legal systems, whereas the former is an attempt to remove striking differences between member states' policies in order to achieve a smoother function of the sector in issue. Provisions on public procurement in many member states have taken the form of ministerial circulars, orders and administrative practices. There is little doubt that the public procurement sector is dominated by national sensibilities that change continuously, thus requiring frequent governmental intervention. Decision-making with respect to regional and social development, anti-cyclical demand management, and employment are less autonomous policy objectives which also dictate the need to observe implementation of EC public procurement directives through administrative practices. On the other hand, statutory implementation of such directives provides for a clearer and more precise regime, as individuals in member states may rely upon legally enforceable rights before national courts in a dispute that falls within the framework of those directives.

The public procurement regime can be classified into the public supplies sector, which is regulated by EEC Directive 70/32 and 77/62 as amended by Directives 80/767 and 88/295 and consolidated by Directive 93/36; the public works sector, which is regulated by Directives 71/304 and 71/305 as amended by Directive 89/440 and consolidated by Directive 93/37; the public utilities sector, which is regulated by Directive 90/531, as amended by Directive 93/38; and the public services sector, which is regulated by Directive 92/50. The principal objective of all public procurement directives derives from the assumption that transparency and improved market information should enhance market efficiency, by ensuring that conditions of competition are not distorted and that contracts are allocated to suppliers and contractors under the conditions which are most favourable for the contracting authorities. The directives are based on three underlying fundamental principles: Community-wide advertising of public contracts above certain thresholds; prohibition of technical specifications capable of discriminating against potential bidders; and application of objective criteria of participation in tendering and award procedures.

The Public Supplies Regime

The transitional period (the period from the establishment of the European Communities until 31 December 1969) witnessed the first attempts to regulate the public procurement sector. For the purpose of giving guidance to Community institutions and member states in the implementation of Articles 52, 53 EECT and 59, 60 EECT, in 1962 the Council of Ministers adopted two *Programmes Generales* for the elimination of existing restrictions on interstate trade. Among the restrictions to be abolished were rules and practices of member states, with respect to foreigners only, which '[e]xclude, limit or impose conditions upon the capacity to submit offers or to participate as main contractors or subcontractors in contract awards by the State or legal persons governed by public law'. Both *Programmes* envisaged a gradual and balanced removal of restrictions based on quotas and the coordination of national procedures for the award of public contracts to nationals of other member states through agencies or branches or directly to persons or undertakings established in other member states.

With respect to the prohibition of quotas and measures having an effect equivalent to quantitative restrictions, in 1966 the Commission introduced Directive 66/683 requiring the elimination of measures prohibiting the use of imported products or prescribing the use of domestic products. However, public supplies contracts were exempted, pending the adoption of a specific directive. Four years later, in 1970 the Commission introduced directive 70/32 on the basis of Article 33(7) EECT, applying the prohibition of measures having an equivalent effect to public procurement. This directive applied to all products of whatever description which were admitted to free circulation within the Community by virtue of Articles 9 and 10 EECT. These were products originating in a member state, and third-country products admitted to free circulation in a member state. It indicated two barriers posed by the state, its territorial authorities and other public corporate bodies, upon procurement of public supplies (articles 3(1) and 3(2), as well as the preamble) – those preventing or inhibiting the supply of imported products and those favouring the supply of domestic products or granting preferential treatment (other than state aids, which must be assessed under the framework of Article 92 EECT and taxation) to domestic suppliers. In addition, the directive (article 3(3)) listed a number of forms of discrimination against foreign goods. Among those were technical specifications, which though applicable to both domestic and imported products, had restrictive effects on trade. The *ratione* and the underlying aim were the same with Directive 66/683, but the very first Community instrument to regulate public supplies contracts (Directive 70/32) came into force when the transitional period had virtually expired, thus rendering Article 30 directly effective. One might question the logic behind that decision.

A possible answer could be that having Article 30 directly effective, after the elapse of the transitional period, the whole directive would have been better implemented into national legal orders; thus Article 30 could have served as a yardstick for its incorporation by member states. On the other hand, this delay on the part of the Community in adopting an instrument regulating public supplies revealed a highly complicated and sensitive regime that was related not only to the free movement of goods, but which expanded further covering aspects in the field of competition and common commercial policy. The most difficult obstacle appeared to be the regulation, under the same legal instrument, of intraterritorial and extraterritorial aspects of the principle of free movement of goods with reference to public supplies. The expiry of the transitional period helped the Community as to the former; having established direct effectiveness of Article 30 EECT within the Common Market, effort was focused on the latter, and that was the extraterritorial application of Community law in respect to public supplies.

In 1977, the Council adopted Directive 77/62 (OJ 1977, L13/1) pursuant to Articles 30 and 100 EECT, concerning the coordination of procedures for the award of public supply contracts. This instrument, which came into force in 1978, was designed to ensure a more effective supervision of compliance with the negative obligations of Article 30 EECT and Directive 70/32 by means of the imposition of a number of positive obligations on purchasing bodies (Article 1(b): contracting authorities specified in Annex I).

The imposition of a positive obligation on a member state by a directive reveals that a margin of discretion as to the forms and methods of the result to be achieved is provided for. Of course, there is no doubt that directives are binding only with respect to the result to be achieved, thus requiring member states to opt for the appropriate methods and forms to implement their provisions into domestic law, but the fact that a directive imposes a positive obligation may affect the direct effectiveness of its provisions, in case of wrongful or non-implementation. Positive obligations, in contrast to negative ones, allot to member states a greater margin of discretion. Member states should abstain from action that hinders a Community aim, but, in addition, they must take all the appropriate measures to enhance the function and operation of achieving that aim. A positive obligation seems to contain two subsequent requirements: that of abstention and that of introduction of further measures to secure the results of the former.

With respect to the direct effectiveness of provisions of directives imposing positive obligations on member states, the court initially was reluctant[1] to accept that the margin of discretion derived from a positive obligation was capable of rendering the provision in question directly effective. Interestingly, in two cases[2] it ruled that even positive obligations contained in a

1. See case 57/65 *Alfons Luttucke v. Hauptzollampt Saarlouis* [1966] ECR 205.
2. Case 28/67 *Firma Molkerei-Zentrale Westfalen/Lippe GmbH v. Haupzollampt Pederborn* [1968] ECR 143; case 13/68 *SpA Salgoil v. Italian Ministry of Foreign Trade* [1968] ECR 453.

directive may produce direct effect, but the situation is far from clear.

The fact that Directive 77/62 imposed a number of positive obligations on member states raised a number of questions as to the direct effectiveness of its provisions. The aim of the directive was that transparency and improved market information should enhance market efficiency by ensuring that conditions of competition were not distorted and that contracts were allocated to suppliers and contractors under the most favourable conditions for the contracting authorities. The strategy was based on three basic principles: (i) Community-wide advertising of contracts; (ii) prohibition of technical specifications capable of discriminating against potential bidders; and (iii) application of objective criteria of participation in tendering and award procedures. However, the scope of the directive was rather limited. It excluded public supplies contracts by transport authorities, the production, distribution, transmission and transport services for water or energy, and telecommunications services. Apparently the main legal reason for this exclusion was that these entities had different legal statuses and operated under different regimes in member states. Some of them were governed by public law, others by private law, while some were in the process of privatization, although the essential control remained in the hands of the state. On the other hand, it could be argued that this was not a valid argument, since the instruments employed for the regulation of such entities were directives, which implement envisaged Community standards into national law, taking into account existing national sensibilities. It appears that the regulation of the public utilities in respect to their purchasing arrangements was rather premature for the time.

Directive 77/62 contained a sort of *de minimis* rule; it was applicable only to public supply contracts with an estimated value net of VAT in excess of EUA (European Units Account) 200,000. Its legal basis (Articles 30 and 100 EECT) rendered it inapplicable to products originating in and supplied by third countries. The directive was also inapplicable to public supplies contracts awarded (i) pursuant to an international agreement between a member state and one or more non-member countries; (ii) pursuant to an international agreement relating to the stationing of troops between undertakings in a member state or a non-member country; and (iii) pursuant to a particular process of an international agreement.

In 1980 Directive 77/62 was amended by Directive 80/767 (OJ 1980, L215/1) in order to take account of the 1979 GATT Agreement on Government Procurement. That Agreement committed the Community to grant better access to suppliers from third countries, through the application of lower thresholds, to central government purchasing and to some defence procurement, than suppliers from the Community enjoyed under directive 77/62. That Agreement became part of Community law as it was approved by Council Decision 80/271 (OJ 1980, L215/1).

In 1984 the Commission's Communication to the Council on public supply contracts revealed an unsatisfactory situation with respect to the implementation of the supplies directives in the legal systems of member states. The list of factors responsible for the lack of success included, *inter alia*:

- failure to advertise contracts in the *Official Journal*, as a result of splitting up of contracts, although improvements had been made in the retrieval of information as the result of the establishment of the TED (Tenders Electronic Daily) data bank;
- ignorance of the relevant rules on the part of contracting authorities, or deliberate omission of these rules;
- excessive use of the exceptions permitting non-competitive tendering (negotiated procedures) instead of open or restricted procedures;
- discriminatory requirements imposed by contracting authorities by means of compliance with national technical standards, to the exclusion of European standards or equivalent standards of other countries;
- unlawful disqualification of suppliers or contractors, or discriminatory use of the award criteria.

The Commission's White Paper on the completion of the internal market reiterated that there was a serious and urgent need for improvement and elaboration of the relevant public procurement directives. In accordance with the Commission's action programme, in 1988 the Council adopted Directive 88/295 (OJ 1988, L127/1) amending all previous supplies directives. The main improvements were:

- open tendering procedures as the norm, negotiated ones being allowed in exceptional circumstances;
- the definition of the types of supplies contracts was widened

and the method of calculation of the thresholds was clarified;

- the exempted sectors were more strictly defined;
- purchasing authorities had to publish in advance information on their annual procurement programmes and their timetable, as well as a notice giving details of the outcome of each award decision;
- the rules on technical standards were brought in line with the new policy on standards which is based on the mutual recognition of national requirements, where the objectives of national legislation are essentially equivalent, and on the process of legislative harmonization of technical standards through non-governmental standardization organizations (CEPT, CEN, CENELEC).

In an attempt to consolidate all previous legislation relating to public supplies and align it in conformity with the relevant directives on public works and public services and the utilities sector, Directive 93/36[3] was adopted in June 1993. The consolidated directives aim at introducing a similar procedural regime in their relevant sectors and at enhancing clarity of some of the previously existing provisions.[4]

The public works regime

The two *Programmes Generales* adopted by the Council for the purpose of guiding Community institutions in the implementation of the provisions of Articles 52, 53, 59 and 62 EEC Treaty, took account of the special features of public works contracts. A gradual and balanced removal of restrictions based on quotas and the coordination of national procedures for awarding public works contracts to nationals of other member states were the main aims envisaged therein.

The issue of public sector activities related to construction contracts after the transitional period was addressed by Directive 71/304 (OJ 1971, L185/1), which required member states to abolish restrictions on participation of non-nationals in public procurement contracts. It came into force after the completion of the transitional period, when Articles 59 and 60 EECT concerning

3. OJ 1993, L199.
4. See P.J. Birkinshaw and C. Bovis, 'Public Procurement: Legislation and Commentary', *Butterworths European Law Service*, 1992.

the freedom to provide services became directly effective, thus leaving few aspects to be implemented by member states. It now serves mainly to list professional trade activities which constitute public works.

The aims envisaged in Articles 52 *et seq.* on the right of establishment and Articles 59 *et seq.* on the freedom to provide services were further enhanced by the adoption of Directive 71/305 (OJ 1971, L185/5), which was the primary vehicle for the opening up of the public works contracts. Based on the prohibition of discriminatory technical specifications, adequate advertising of contracts, the fixing of objective participation criteria and a joint supervision procedure both by member states' authorities and the EC Commission to ensure observation of these principles, it sought the coordination of national procedures in the award of public works contracts. The directive's major objective was the establishment and enhancement of a transparent regime in the public works sector, where conditions of undistorted competition would ensure that contracts are allocated to contractors under the most favourable terms for the contracting authorities. Like the Supplies Directive 77/62, Directive 71/305 had a limited aim. It did not introduce new tendering procedures, nor were existing national procedures and practices replaced by a set of Community rules. Member states remained free to maintain or adopt substantive and procedural rules, on condition that they should comply with all the relevant provisions of Community law and, in particular, the prohibitions following from the principles laid down in the Treaty in regard to the right of establishment and the freedom to provide services.[5]

The concept of contract under the first works directive was very extensive, covering contracts concluded in writing between a contractor and a contracting authority for pecuniary interest concerning either the execution alone or both the execution alone and design of works related to building or civil engineering activities listed in class 50 of the NACE Classification,[6] or the execution by whatever means of a work corresponding to the requirements specified by the contracting authority. The above formula was wide enough to embrace modern forms of contract such as project developing contracts, management contracts and

5. See cases 27, 28, 29/86, *CEI* and *Bellini* [1987] ECR 3347.
6. General Industrial Classification of Economic Activities within the European Communities; see Annex II, directive 71/305.

concession contracts. Concession contracts are for public works projects under which the consideration for the works consists in a franchise (concession) to operate the completed works, or in a franchise plus payment. The initial Works Directive 71/305 did not apply to concession contracts, except in the case that the concessionaire was a public authority covered by the directive. In such a situation, the works subcontracted to third parties would be fully subject to its provisions. In any other case, the only provisions of the directive were that the concessionaire should not discriminate on grounds of nationality when it itself awarded contracts to third parties. The regulation of concession contracts was introduced almost two decades later by Directive 89/440 amending Directive 71/305. In fact, it incorporated the Voluntary Code of Practice which was adopted by the Representatives of member states meeting within the Council in 1971.[7] The Code was a non-binding instrument and contained rules on the advertising of contracts and the principle that contracting authorities awarding the principal contract to a concessionaire were to require the concessionaire to subcontract to third parties at least 30 per cent of the total work provided for by the principal contract. Obviously, these requirements could not easily be incorporated in a binding instrument such as Directive 89/440; thus a relaxation of member states' commitments occurs therein. As a result, the coordination rules of the latter apply to concession contracts only in respect of advertising. The directive's rules on tendering procedures, suitability criteria and award procedures and technical specifications were inapplicable. Interestingly, Article 3(3) of Directive 71/305 on the prohibition of discrimination on grounds of nationality by a concessionaire awarding subcontracts has disappeared from the text of the amending Directive 89/440. The reason could be that by the end of the transitional period Articles 7, 48, 52, 59 and 119 EECT were directly effective and, in addition, their horizontal direct effect had been pronounced by the European Court of Justice.[8]

The definition of contractors comprised any legal or natural person involved in construction activities, and for the purposes of the directive, the contracting authority might impose a requirement as to the form and legal status of the contractor that

7. OJ 1971, C82/13.
8. See case 36/74 *Walrave and Koch v. Association Union Cycliste International et al.*, (1974) ECR 1423; case 43/75, *Drefenne v. SABENA* (1976) ECR 473.

won the award. As far as contracting authorities were concerned, their definition was very wide, covering bodies governed by public law – defined as being any body 'established for the specific purpose of meeting needs in the general interest and not having an industrial or commercial character, which has legal personality and is financed for the most part by the State or is subject to management supervision by the latter.' This definition resembles the court's ruling on state-controlled enterprises in *Marshall v. Southampton and South West Hampshire Area Health Authority* (case 152/84 [1986] ECR 723). There is a list of such bodies in Annex I of Directive 71/305, which is not an exhaustive one like that in the supplies directive, and member states were under an obligation to notify the Commission of any changes in that list.

Works contracts in the utilities and defence sectors and those awarded in pursuance of certain international agreements were explicitly excluded by virtue of Articles 4 and 5 of the directive. These provisions were identical in effect to the corresponding ones of the supplies directive. This revealed the fact that public contracts under the framework of the works directive covered mainly construction projects in the education, health, sports and leisure facilities sectors, inasmuch as the state or regional or local authorities undertake such projects. In the event that certain entities involved in this sort of activity (e.g. a hospital or a university) might enjoy considerable independence from the state or local government, as to the undertaking of works contracts, Directive 71/305 was inapplicable to them, since they were not included in its Annex I as bodies governed by public law for the purposes of the directive in question. This seems to have limited the scope of the directive to cases where the state or local government had direct control over the above-mentioned entities. Given the fact that works contracts in the utilities sectors were also excluded from the framework of the directive, its applicability covered a rather modest portion of the construction sector. In order to overcome this apparently undesirable result, the amending Directive 89/440 provides for an obligation upon member states to ensure compliance with its provisions when they subsidize directly by more than 50 per cent, a works contract awarded by an entity involved in activities relating to certain civil engineering works and to the building of hospitals, sports recreation and leisure facilities, school and university buildings and buildings used for administrative purposes. These conditions seem not to impose a heavy duty on member states, as only direct subsidies trigger the applicability of the directive. Indirect ways of subsidizing the entities in question, such as tax exemptions, guaranteed loans, or provision of land free of charge, render it inapplicable.

It should be noted that under both the original supplies and works directives, preference schemes in the award of contracts were allowed. Such schemes required the application of award criteria based on considerations other than the lowest price or the most economically advantageous tender, which are common in both regimes. However, preferences could only be compatible with Community law in as much as they did not run contrary to the principle of free movement of goods (Article 30 EECT *et seq.*) and to competition law considerations in respect of state aid.[9] Preference schemes have been abolished since the completition of the internal market at the end of 1992.

In 1993, the Council enacted a directive with a view to consolidating all existing legislation in the field of public works. The consolidated Directive 93/37[10] embraces all relevant Community legislation relating to public works, with some minor amendments and clarifications of the existing provisions of Directive 89/440.

The public utilities regime

As previously mentioned, both supplies and works contracts in the transport, water, energy and telecommunications sectors were excluded from the relevant supplies and works directives. The exclusion of the above-mentioned sectors from the framework of the supplies directives (77/62 and 88/295) had been attributed to the fact that the authorities entrusted with the operation of public utilities had been subject to differing legal status in member states, varying from completely state-controlled enterprises to private firms. With respect to works directives, the above justification appears valid, although the apparent connection between construction projects and the excluded sectors leads to the conclusion that Directives 71/305 and 89/440 have very limited application.

9. See the Commission's communication on the *Regional and Social Aspects of public procurement*, where it gives an overview of the preference schemes still existing in member states, COM(89) 400 fin.

10. Directive 93/37, OJ 1993, L199.

As far as supplies contracts were concerned, a convincing reason behind the exclusion of these sectors is that the projects covered therein could not fall within the cost thresholds of Directives 77/62 and 88/295. Energy, telecommunications, transport and, to a lesser extent, the water industry, are technical sectors requiring state-of-the-art technology (especially telecommunications and energy). The cost thresholds in such contracts are very high in comparison with (simple) supplies ones (ECU 400,000 for water, energy and transport supplies and ECU 600,000 for telecommunications supplies), so the only way these sectors could be brought within Directive 77/62 would have been either to increase the cost thresholds (ECU 200,000) of the supplies contracts to such a level as to catch a substantial amount of contracts of the excluded sectors, or on the other hand, to lower the envisaged cost thresholds of contracts in telecommunications, energy, transport and water industry sectors to the level of the (simple) supplies ones. Either option would have resulted in a very undesirable situation; if the first option was chosen, the bulk of supplies contracts would have escaped from the framework of Directive 77/62. On the other hand, squeezing the thresholds of the excluded sectors to ECU 200,000 would have effectively eliminated the *de minimis* rule for those sectors. A *de minimis* rule is a *conditio sine qua non* where quantitative criteria for regulation of a sector are chosen.

With respect to works contracts, the exclusion of the telecommunications, transport, energy and water industry sectors from Directives 71/305 and 89/440 could be justified, rather, due to the different legal statuses of the entities in question in the member states. If a private firm operating in the above sectors were to be involved in a construction project, the works directives would be inapplicable, as private firms were not included among the contracting authorities specified in Annex I (bodies governed by public law). To cover both private and public-controlled entities operating in the relevant utilities sectors, the works directives should have expanded the definition of contracting authorities; but this would have resulted in an internal disturbance of the operation of the directives, which are envisaged as regulating construction project awards exclusively by the state or local government or bodies governed by public law. Thus, the only viable and reasonable solution was to introduce a separate instrument, applying the same principles as those found in

Directive 77/62, in order to regulate the transport, telecommunications, energy and water sectors.

The Commission was requested by the Council to follow the progress of the CEPT proceedings[11] on harmonization in the field of telecommunications and to submit to the latter a timetable for measures ensuring effective competition in the field of supply contracts awarded for telecommunications services. The Commission, in its recommendations on telecommunications, also expressed its desire to ensure that the objective of an open market, in particular for suppliers within the Community, was being achieved without undesirable consequences for the pattern of Community trade with non-member countries. In its Communication to the Council of 1984 on public supply contracts and its White Paper on the completion of the internal market, the Commission reiterated the need to liberalize the so far excluded sectors, particularly telecommunications.

The European Parliament's Committee on Economic and Monetary Affairs and Industrial Policy presented a report in the European Parliament stressing the need for extension of the scope of the supplies directives to cover excluded sectors. In its Resolution the Parliament approved all the Commission's and Council's actions so far, and requested them to submit a proposal for a directive to govern the excluded sectors. The Council, in its Recommendation 84/550, shared the Commission's considerations as to the opening of access to public telecommunications contracts, providing that governments of member states should offer opportunities for Community undertakings to tender on a non-discriminatory basis for the supply of specified telecommunications equipment and should also report to the Commission on implementing measures and practical effects. In 1988 the Commission issued Directive 88/301 on competition in the markets in telecommunications terminal equipment.

Finally, in 1990 the Council adopted Directive 90/531[12] on the procurement procedures of entities operating in the water, energy, transport and telecommunications sectors. The regime imposed is rather similar to the supplies directives, with some important

11. CEPT is the European Conference of Postal and Telecommunications Administrations, established in Montreux in 1959 and aiming at closer relations between member administration to improve their administrative and technical services; OJ 1977, C11/3.

12. OJ 1990, L297.

differences as to the flexibility given to the contracting authorities over the choice of methods to be used to make the award process competitive. The directive has provided different implementing periods for Spain, Greece and Portugal: Spain had to implement its provisions by 1 January, 1996 whereas Greece and Portugal had until 1 January 1998. The delay in the uniform implementation of the utilities directive could be attributed to the preparations needed for the integration of the public utilities sectors in the respective countries. The utilities directive has been amended by Directive 93/38,[13] which mainly incorporates the newly enacted Public Services Directive 92/50[14] into the utilities regime.

The legislative background of the utilities directive and the experience of the regulation of public utilities procurement justify the high complexity of the regime. The fact that public utilities often have an unclear legal status, or their legal nature varies within the member states' legal systems, has obviously rendered it difficult to introduce a single legal instrument to regulate their purchasing activities, although the prolonged delay should be attributed to other factors. It may be recalled that public utilities absorb the vast majority of high technology equipment designated to the public sector. Protectionism in strategic industrial sectors has been pursued through preferential purchasing with a view to either sustaining the relevant industries or to assisting the development of infant industries in member states. The regulation of utilities purchasing not only has had to overcome the significant legislative barriers accountable to their nature but also the abandoning of individual industrial policies of member states through strategic procurement. In addition to these constraints, the fear of an uncontrolled flow of direct investment which would target vulnerable European-based high technology industries and the subsequent possible increase in takeovers and acquisitions, mainly from Japanese and American predators, poured cold water on the attempts of European institutions to integrate utilities procurement within the Common Market.

The utilities directive has been a most radical approach to the public sector integration in Europe and its enactment coincided with the envisaged international liberalization of public procurement during the Uruguay GATT negotiations. One could

13. OJ 1993, L199.
14. OJ 92/50, OJ 1992, L209.

question the adoption of such a strategy by European institutions, particularly bearing in mind the vulnerability of Europes high-tech industry in comparison with those in the USA and Japan. However, the GATT regime has introduced a new era – to the extent that highly protectionist countries like the USA and Japan must abolish their buy-national laws and policies and, on a reciprocal basis, open their public markets to international competition.

The ambit of the utilities directive and its field of application appear more complicated than those in the supplies and works directives, although the internal legal structure of each of the three directives is very similar. Articles 1 and 2 form the broad framework of the directive's application, by providing various definitions and the scope of some preliminary exemptions. The utilities directive devotes a substantial amount of provisions in an attempt to exempt from its application certain contracts or activities that have been deemed ineligible for community-wide regulation.

Apart from the normal exemptions under the grounds of defence and security and confidentiality, the major exemptions are provided for under Articles 1 and 2. Radio and television broadcasting have not been classified as telecommunication activities and have been specifically excluded from the ambit of the directive by virtue of Article 2. Also, bus transport services to the public are excluded on condition that their providers operate under a regime of competitive conditions, which means that other potential contractors or suppliers of similar services are allowed to enter the relevant geographical and product markets and compete against the existing utilities provider (Article 2 (4)). A similar rule applies to telecommunication services which operate within a competitive market (Article 8).

Under the same Article 2 special exemptions are also provided to private entities supplying gas, heat, drinking water and electricity. Although the wording and spirit of the directive cover private entities operating under exclusive and special rights in the utilities sectors, under certain conditions, these entities can be expemted from the application of the rules of the directive. In the case of the production of drinking water and electricity, if a private entity is able to show that it does so for its own purposes, which are not related to the provision of drinking water or electricity to the public, it is exempt. Similarly, if a private entity is able to show that it supplies to the public network drinking water or electricity which is destined for its own consumption, and that the total so supplied to the network is not more than 30 per cent of the total produced by that network in any one year over a three-year period, it also is exempt.

In the case of gas and heat supplies, if the production by a private entity is related to an activity other than the supply to a network for public consumption, then these entities are also exempt. Similarly, if the supply of gas and heat by a private entity to a public network relates to economic exploitation only which is not considered to be the main activity of the privare entity and does not exceed 20% of the firm's turnover in any one year, taking an average of the preceding three years and the current year, then such entity is also exempt. These exemptions predominanly cover entities which have research and development as their main objective in the relevant utilities sector, or which do not play a major role in supplying public networks with water or energy.[15]

There are also exemptions for entities exploring for gas, oil, coal and other solid fuels, under Article 3. Entities operating in these sectors will not be regarded as having an exclusive right, provided that certain conditions are fulfilled. These conditions are cumulative and stipulate that, when an exploitation right is granted to the entity in question, the latter is exempt from the utilities directives provided that other bodies are able to compete for the same exclusive rights under free competition; that the financial and technical criteria to be used in awarding rights are clearly spelt out before the award is made; that the objective criteria are specified as to the way in which exploitation is to be carried out; that these criteria are published before requests for tenders are made, and applied in a non-discriminatory way; that all operating obligations, royalty and capital and revenue participation agreements are published in advance; and finally, that contracting authorities are not required to provide information on their procurement intentions except at the request of national authorities. Furthermore, member states have to ensure that these exempted bodies apply, at least, the principles of non-discrimination and competition. They are obliged to provide a report to the European Commission on request about such

15. See N. O'Loan, 'Implementation of Directive 90/531 and Directive 92/50 in the United Kingdom', *Public Procurement Law Review*, 1993, p. 29. Also, A. Cox, *Public Procurement in the European Community:The single market rules and the enforcement regime after 1992,* Erlsgate Press, 1993.

contracts. However, this requirement is less stringent than the mandatory reporting rules in the supply and works directives. It should be mentioned that the utilities directive does not apply to concession contracts granted to entities operating in utilities sectors, awarded prior to the coming into force of the directive. All exemption provisions within the utilities directive are subject to assessment in the light of the four-year overall review of the process.

Other exemptions cover entities in the relevant sectors which can demonstrate that their service and network associated contracts are not related to the specific supply and works functions specified in the directive, or if they are so related, that they take place in a non-member state and are not using a European public network or physical area. The member states are under an obligation to inform the European Commission, on request, of the cases when these exemptions have been allowed. There are also provisions which allow for resale and hire contracts to third parties to be exempt when the awarding body does not possess an exclusive or special right to hire or sell the subject of the contract, and there is already competition in the market from other suppliers or producers to provide the commodity or service to third parties. Similar relaxed reporting and monitoring requirements are found in Article 8, which applies to telecommunication exemptions.

Another set of significant exemptions is provided for water authorities under Article 9. Under this provision water authorities specified in Annex 1 are specifically exempt from the rules when they purchase water. They are, however, covered by the directive when they purchase other supply and construction products. Similarly, there are specific exemptions for the electricity, gas and heat, oil and coal and other solid fuels entities outlined in Annexes II, III, IV and V, but only when they award contracts for the supply of energy or for fuels for the production of energy. For all other relevant contracts these bodies are included in the rules. These exemptions were provided because of the need to allow contracting authorities to buy from local sources of supply, which may not always be the cheapest, but which are important on the basis of regional development policies or environmental grounds, and because these purchases are central to the entities' operations and not part of the normal supply and works procurement process.

Finally, specific exemptions under the utilities directive are provided for those carriers of passengers and providers of transport services by air and by sea. In the preamble of the directive it is stated that, under a series of measures adopted in 1987 with a view to introducing more competition between firms providing public air services, it was decided to exempt such carriers from the scope of the legislation. Similarly, because shipping has been subject to severe competitive pressures, it was decided to exempt certain types of contracts from the directive.

The utilities directive intends to open up procurement practices in the four previously excluded sectors, mainly to EC-wide competition. With respect to goods (and services) originating in third countries, things are more complicated. A product from outside the Community, in order to be subject to a public contract regulated by one of the EC public procurement directives, must lawfully be put in free circulation in at least one member state. Except where there has been an international agreement which grants comparable and effective access for Community undertakings to public markets of a third country (the reciprocity principle), Article 29 renders it possible for European contracting authorities in the utilities sector to reject offers from outsde the Community, and requires Community preference where Community offers are equivalent to offers from third countries (deemed such where the price difference does not exceed 3%). With reference to an international agreement granting access to public markets, the utilities directive opens the door for the application of the GATT Agreement on Government Procurement in the utilities sector.

The public services regime

While the liberalization of trade, as envisaged in international agreements such as the GATT or in supranational organizations such as the European Communities, embraces primarily the free movement of goods, provisions regulating the provision of services are often described as inadequate. Modern economies have witnessed a shift in trade patterns from product manufacturing industries to markets where the provision of services is the predominant sector of the industry. The lack of regulation of services at a global level has given rise to economic controversies. Trade wars have been taking place and the international legal community is currently attempting to adopt measures towards regulation of trade in services within the context of the GATT Uruguay Round of multilateral trade negotiations.

In line with the above considerations, Directive 92/50[16] on the award procedures relating to public services contracts attempts to pave the way for liberalization of services in public markets. The directive follows the same principles with the rest of the Community's legislation on public procurement, that is compulsory Community-wide advertising of public contracts, prohibition of technical specification capable of discriminating against potential bidders and uniform application of objective criteria of participation in tendering and award procedures. The services directive has introduced a special type of award procedure, namely 'design contests', with reference to planning projects. According to Article 1 (g), design contests are those national procedures which enable the contracting authority to acquire in the fields of area planning, town planning, architecture and civil engineering, a plan or a design selected by a jury, after being put out to competition with or without the award of prizes.

Under the services directive, public services contracts are contracts which have as their object the provision of services classified in the Common Product Classification (CPC) nomenclature of the United Nations, as a nomenclature for classification of services at Community level is lacking. The United Nations' Common Product Classification covers almost every conceivable service an undertaking may provide, although the services description is rather plain.

The services directive is the first legal instrument to attempt to open the increasingly important public services sector to intra-Community competition. It should be mentioned that the directives on public supplies, public works and utilities contain provisions whereby the provision of services is regarded as ancillary to the main contract under their regime, provided the value of the services is less than the value of the supplies or works. Such services are covered by the relevant directive.

Specific services contracts are excluded from the scope of the services directive. It should be mentioned that not all of these specific exclusions are listed in the amended Utilities Directive 93/38, because they would not, in any event, fall within the ambit of a defined activity. Apart from those contracts which are covered

16. OJ 92/50, OJ 1992, L209.

by the relevant provisions of the works, supplies and utilities directives, and therefore not considered as services, the other contracts excluded from the services directive and amended Utilities Directive 93/38 are:

(1) contracts for the acquisition or rental, by whatever financial means, of land, existing buildings, or other immoveable property or concerning rights thereon. However, financial service contracts concluded at the same time as, before or after the contract of acquisition or rental, in whatever form, will be subject to the directive;
(2) contracts for the acquisition, development, production or co-production of programme material by broadcasters and contracts for broadcasting time. This includes the purchase of, on the one hand, services producing audio-visual works such as films, videos and sound recording, including advertising and, on the other hand, broadcasting time (transmission by air, satellite or cable). In principle, these services would be covered but are given derogations in so far as they are connected with broadcasting activities;[17]
(3) contracts for voice telephony, telex, radiotelephony, paging and satellite services;
(4) contracts for arbitration and conciliation services;
(5) contracts for financial services in connection with the issue, sale, purchase or transfer of securities or other financial instruments, and central bank services. This refers to contracts which constitute transactions concerning shares, for example. In the public sector, it will also include within the derogation contracts awarded to financial intermediaries to arrange such transactions because these are specifically excluded from the scope of investment services (Category 6 of annex IA). However, this exclusion does not appear in the utilities directive so that contracts for the services of intermediaries who will make the arrangements for such transactions will be subject to the provisions of the utilities directive. The choice of such intermediaries is often difficult in practice since it is quite often made on the basis of the perceived quality of the intermediary or on references from existing clients and past experience. This choice will be made no easier by the

17. See P. Armin-Trepte, 'Public procurement in the EC', *CCH Europe,* 1993, p. 101.

application of the procurement rules which do not necessarily best fit such services;[18]

(6) employment contracts;

(7) research and development service contracts other than those where the benefits accrue exclusively to the contracting authority for its use in the conduct of its own affairs, on condition that the service provided is mostly remunerated by the contracting authority.

Research and development services contracts are covered in identical terms in both directives. The exclusion of such contracts under both the services and the utilities directives lies in the assumption that research and development projects should not be financed by public funds. However, where research and development contracts are covered by the procurement rules, a provision in the utilities directive allows a contracting entity to award a contract without a prior call for competition where it is purely for the purpose of research, experiment, study or development and not for the purpose of ensuring profit or of recovering research and development costs and in so far as the award of such contract does not prejudice the competitive award of subsequent contracts which have in particular these purposes.

Interestingly, service concessions, although included in the draft directive, have been excluded from the provisions of directive 92/50. The exclusion of service concessions falls short of the aspirations to regulate concession contracts for the public sector under the works directive and breaks the consistency in the two legal instruments. The reasons for the exclusion of service concessions from the regulatory regime of public procurement could be attributed to the different legal requirements in member states to delegate powers to concessionaires. The delegation of services by public authorities to private undertakings in some member states runs contrary to constitutional provisions.

The directive adopts a two-tier approach in classifying services procured by contracting authorities. This classification is based on 'priority' and 'non-priority' lists of services, according to the relative value of such services in intra-Community trade.

18. See de Graaf 'The political agreement on a common position concerning the utilities services directive', *Public Procurement Law Review*, 1992, p. 473; also P. Armin-Trepte, *op. cit.* n. 17 above.

Priority services. These include:

maintenance and repair services;
land transport services (except for rail transport services), including armoured car services and courier services, except transport of mail,
air transport services of passengers and freight, except transport of mail;
transport of mail by land and by air;
telecommunications services (except voice telephony, telex, radiotelephony, paging and satellite services);
financial services, including (i) insurance services, (ii) banking and investment services (except contracts for financial services in connection with the issue, sale, purchase or transfer of securities or other financial instruments, and central bank services);
computer and related services;
research and development services;
accounting, auditing and book-keeping services;
market research and public opinion polling services;
management consultant services (except arbitration and conciliation services) and related services;
architectural services;
engineering services and integrated engineering services;
urban planning and landscape architectural services;
related scientific and technical consulting services;
technical testing and analysis services;
advertising services;
building-cleaning services on a fee or contract basis;
publishing and printing services on a fee or contract basis;
sewage and refuse disposal services;
sanitation and similar services.

Non-priority services. These include:

hotel and restaurant services;
rail transport services;
water transport services;
supporting and auxiliary transport services;
legal services;
personnel placement and supply services;
investigation and security services;
education and vocational education services;
health and social services;
recreational, cultural and sporting services.

The division is not permanent and the European Commission has the situation under constant review, by assessing the performance of 'non-priority' services sectors. The two-tier approach, in practical terms, means that the award of priority services contracts are subject to the rigorous regime of the public procurement directives (advertisement, selection of tenderers, award procedures, award criteria), whereas the award of non-priority services contracts must follow the basic rules of non-discrimination and publicity of the results of the award.

Compliance and enforcement of public procurement legislation

The compliance directives

In the absence of specific primary Community legislation laying down remedies available to individuals at national level in case of infringement of Community law, two questions arise: the first is whether an infringement of a directly effective primary or secondary Community provision may be used by individuals before national courts as grounds for an action for damages against the state; the second question approaches the problem from a slightly different perspective: that the infringed provision does not produce direct effect. Is, then, the state liable toward individuals? Can they seek compensation from the state for its infringement and its wrongful implementation of Community law?

In public procurement cases, Article 30 of the EEC Treaty establishing the free movement of goods and Article 52 concerning the right of establishment, both have direct effect.[19] Also, the European Court of Justice has recognized that specific (substantive) provisions of the relevant directives produce direct effect. There are also cases in which national courts have considered the award of compensation to individuals who suffered damages due to a mere breach of Community law.[20] More

19. This occurred at the end of the transitional period (31 December 1969); see also cases 2/74 *Reyners v. Belgian State* [1974] ECR 631 and 33/74 *Van Bisbergen v. Bestuur van de Bedrijfsvereninging voor de Metaalinijverheid* [1974] ECR 1299.

20. Case 213/89 *The Queen v. Minister of Agriculture Fisheries and Food* [1990] I ECR 2433; also case 14/68 *Wilhem v. Bundeskartellampt* [1969] ECR 1 at 27; case 78/70 *Deutche Grammophon GmbH v. Metro-SB Grossmarkte GmbH* [1971] ECR 1 at 31; case 44/84 *Hurd v. Jones* [1986] ECR 29.

intriguing are those cases before national courts where infringement of Community law has already been pronounced directly by the Court of Justice through a proceeding under Article 169 EECT. In these cases, national courts are confronted with state legislation, the incompatibility of which with Community law has unequivocally and authoritatively been declared by the ECJ. Is the existence of incompatible state legislation a ground for an action for damages before national courts?

The whole matter goes further to the question as to whether the ECJ can require the courts of the member states to make declarations of invalidity in respect of national legislation found to infringe Community law or to make declaration of awards of damages to the victims. By virtue of Article 171 EECT, the ECJ found in the *Waterkeyn* case[21] that national courts are bound to draw the 'necessary inferences' from judgments under Article 169 EECT. What is meant by this term is not clear. In the *Waterkeyn* case, the ECJ did not expressly require national courts to declare invalid a national law or administrative rule that violates directly effective primary or secondary Community legislation. On the other hand, there is a strong suggestion, in the same case, that such measures should be considered invalid.

The assertion of a national rule that violates Community law as valid, probably justified by public interest, would leave individuals with the possibility of being compensated only through judicial review based on the system of no-fault liability, where a wrongful act is not required. This appears to be contrary to the principles of good faith and legitimate expectation, and far removed from the spirit of the Treaty. On the other hand, if national courts recognize the unlawful nature of an infringement of Community law as such, that should, normally, open the door for compensation on the basis of fault.

As far as the Community's non-contractual liability is concerned, the Court of Justice seems to be reluctant to consider that the unlawfulness of European institutions' decisions is, in itself, sufficient to establish the Community's liability. Indeed, the criterion for Community institutions to be held liable for compensation, apart from the actual damage suffered by an individual and the causal link between that damage and the alleged unlawful act of the institution in question,[22] is the sufficiently

21. Cases 314-316/81 and 82 *Procureur de la Republique et al. v. Waterkeyn* [1982] ECR 4337.
22. Case 4/69 *Alfons Lutticke v. Commission* [1971] ECR 325.

flagrant violation of a superior rule of law for the protection of individuals.[23]

In the light of the ECJ's approach towards the Community's non-contractual liability, national courts face the dilemma of whether to limit their protection to individuals to the unenforceability and the setting aside of national legislation that is inconsistent with the Rome Treaty, and to the making of an order for the restitution of sums exacted in breach of Community law, or to expand the above-mentioned protection by recognizing the right to receive compensation for damage sustained as a result of an infringement of Community law.

With respect to the second question, that of the possibility of relying upon a provision of Community law that does not have direct effect, as ground for an action for damages against the state before national courts, the ECJ in one of its most important recent judgments[24] answered in the affirmative. The cases referred to it concerned the non-implementation by Italy of an EEC directive on the protection of employees in the event of the insolvency of their employer, and reached the court through a reference under Article 177 EECT. The questions the court faced, at the request of national courts, were (i) whether provisions of the directive in question (80/987) were capable of producing direct effect, thus being relied upon by individuals, and (ii) the above being answered in the negative, whether individuals had a right to receive compensation from the member state for the negative effects of its failure to implement the directive.

The court found that the provisions of the directive were not sufficiently clear, precise and unconditional to produce direct effect, thus answering the first question in the negative. In considering whether an individual has a right to be compensated by a state that has failed to implement a directive, the Court held that in principle, an individual is entitled to compensation in such circumstances.[25] In order to found state liability, it relied on Article 5 of the EEC Treaty concerning the principle of Community loyalty and solidarity, which provides that member states are under an obligation to take all the necessary measures to ensure

23. Case 5/71 *Aktien-Zuckerfabrik Schoppenstedt v. Council* [1971] ECR 975 at 984.
24. Judgment on the joint cases 6/90 and 9/90 (*Francovich and Bonifaci v. Italian Republic*).
25. See also case 213/89 *The Queen v.Minister of Agriculture Fisheries and Food* [1990] ECR I-2433.

that Community law is properly applied. It has been held by the ECJ[26] that Article 5 EECT (especially its negative obligation) is capable of producing direct effect, but only in conjunction with other substantive Treaty provisions or in circum- stances in which this obligation is further developed in implementing legislation or through case law. Based on the above considerations, as well as on the doctrine of the useful effect (*effet utile*) of Community rules and the rights being acknowledged therein, and which would be weakened if individuals were not provided with the possibility of compensation in the case of their rights being affected by a violation of Community law by a member state, the court proceeded further and examined the specific conditions that should be met in order for an individual suffering damages to be entitled to compensation by the defaulting state.

Three conditions should be fulfilled: first, the result required by the directive must involve the granting of rights to individuals; secondly, these rights must be identifiable on the basis of the provisions of the directive; and thirdly, there must be a clear causal link between the breach of its obligations by the member state and the damage suffered by the individual concerned. The above conditions being met, then an individual may benefit from a right to compensation at national level based on Community law which is not directly effective. The amount of compensation payable should be determined by national courts in accordance with relevant domestic legislation. The *Francovich* judgment was a landmark decision with respect to state liability under Community law. Individuals may rely upon Community law which does not produce direct effect before their national courts. The Court of Justice laid down the required conditions for the admissibility of an action for damages before national courts submitted by an individual claiming damages against a member state which has failed to implement a directive, thereby injuring a right conferred therein. How strict the national courts will be when confronted with such actions remains to be seen in due course. Obviously, harmonization of domestic provisions on award of compensation will be required.

What appears to be common in the two systems of liability (Community non-contractual and state liability) is the importance

26. Case 14/68 *Wilhem v. Bundeskartellampt* [1969] ECR 1 at 27; case 78/70 *Deutche Grammophon GmbH v. Metro-SB Grossmarkte GmbH* [1971] ECR 1 at 31; case 44/84 *Hurd v. Jones* [1986] ECR 29.

that is given to the individual. According to the judgment of the court in the *Francovich* case,[27] the individual must be granted rights conferred by the directive itself. This means that member states and their competent national authorities may not have any discretion in determining the content and extent of such rights. Here, it should be recalled that lack of discretion in the hands of a member state is perhaps the most fundamental condition for the direct effect of provisions of directives. Thus, the relevant provisions of the directive should be close to producing direct effect, being deprived of it due to their conditionality or to their insufficient clarity and precision. On the other hand, Community liability occurs when a rule of law for the protection of individuals has been violated. The latter condition indicates the extent of the legal interest of the individual seeking compensation by the Community. That interest approaches the individual and direct concern required in Article 173(2) EECT, when individuals seek judicial review of regulations *stricto sensu* and directives. The Court of Justice is extremely strict when considering an action for damages brought by an individual against a Community institution under Article 215(2) EECT. Community liability must fulfil the draconian condition of a sufficiently flagrant violation (mostly a qualitative criterion indicating the manifest and grave disregard of the limits of a state's powers)[28] of a superior rule of law for the protection of individuals. Furthermore, the injury resulting from that violation must involve particular economic policy choices.

As many provisions of Community legislation concerning public procurement (directives) are deemed to produce direct effect, the question of whether an infringement of them can be considered as a sufficient ground for an action for damages at national level, combines with the duty of national courts to afford an effective protection mechanism (remedies) of the rights conferred on individuals by directly effective Community law.

In an attempt to provide an answer to these questions, the Council enacted a directive on the harmonization of laws, regulations and administrative provisions relating to the application of review procedures to the award of public works and

27. See joint cases 6/90 and 9/90, *Francovich and Bonifaci v. Italian Republic* [1993] ECR 61.
28. Cases 83 and 94/76 and 4,15,40/77 *Bayerische HNL Vermehrungsbetreibe GmbH v. Council and Commission* [1978] ECR 1209 at 1224-1225.

public supply contracts (Dir 89/665 EEC).[29] In addition, directive 92/13[30] extends the remedies and review procedures covered by directive 89/665 to the water, energy, transport and telecommunication sectors.

Both directives have been based on Article 100A EECT. Some questions arise as to whether this article is the proper legal basis. The first question is whether Article 100A covers approximation of procedural remedies. It could be argued that it is not necessary to harmonize or to approximate procedural remedies, since it is the general duty of member states under Article 5 EECT to ensure the fulfilment of Community obligations. On the other hand, Article 100A contains no express or implied limitation to the approximation of substantive rules of law, in the framework of the completion of an internal market.

The second question relates to the power of national courts or administrative bodies to suspend a procedure or to set aside a decision in respect of the award of a contract. It is not clear whether these tasks and powers can be granted through Article 100A without requiring the addition of Article 235 of EECT. However, it should be admitted that the unanimous decision-making required therein could not be easily achieved, and from a political point of view, the qualified majority provided for in Article 100A EC appears much more desirable.

The scope of the compliance directives

According to Article 1 of Directive 89/665 and Article 1 of Directive 93/13, member states shall ensure effective and rapid review of decisions taken by contracting authorities which infringe public procurement provisions. Undertakings seeking relief from damages in the context of a procedure for the award of a contract should not be treated differently under national rules implementing European public procurement laws and under other national rules. This means that the measures to be taken concerning the review procedures should be similar to national review proceedings, without any discriminatory character.

Any person having or having had an interest in obtaining a particular public supply or public works contract and who has been or risks being harmed by an alleged infringement of public

29. OJ 1989, L395.
30. OJ 1992, L76/7.

procurement provision shall be entitled to seek review before national courts. This is laid down in the third paragraph of Article 1 of Directive 89/665 and in Article 3 of Directive 92/13, and in both cases is followed by a stand-still provision concerning the prior notification by the person seeking review to the contracting authority of the alleged infringement and of his intention to seek review. However, with respect to admissibility aspects, there is no qualitative or quantitative definition of the interest of a person in obtaining a public contract. As to the element of potential harm by an infringement of public procurement provisions, it should be cumulative with the first element, that of interest. The prior notification should intend to exhaust any possibility of amicable settlement before the parties have recourse to national courts.

Where the Compliance directive in the utilities sectors is really novel is in its Chapter 2. Member states are required to give the contracting entities the option of having their purchasing procedures and practices attested by persons authorized by law to exercise this function. Indeed, this attestation mechanism may investigate in advance possible irregularities identified in the award of a public contract and allow the contracting authorities to correct them. The latter may include the attestation statement in the notice inviting tenders published in the *Official Journal*. The system appears flexible and cost-efficient and may prevent wasteful litigation. Quite promisingly, the attestation procedure under directive 92/13 will be the essential requirement for the development of European standards of attestation. A more detailed analysis of the compliance directives follows in Chapter 4.

The operation of the public procurement directives

The applicability of the directives: definitions

Contracting authorities

Under the supplies, works and services directives, the term 'contracting authorities' include the state and its organs, interpreted in functional terms. It also covers bodies governed by public law, a legal category which must satisfy a set of cumulative criteria for a contracting authority to be characterized as such. The body must be established for the specific purpose of meeting needs in the general interest not having an industrial or commercial character; it must have legal personality; it must be financed, for the most part, by the state or regional or local authorities; it must be subject to management and supervision by those bodies. The utilities directive also uses the term 'bodies governed by public law' for the contracting entities operating in the relevant sectors. A second category of contracting authorities under the utilities directive includes public undertakings. The term indicates any undertaking over which the state may exercise direct or indirect dominant influence by means of ownership, or of finacial participation therein, or of laws and regulations which govern it. Dominant influence can be exercised in the form of majority holding of the undertaking's subscribed capital, in the form of majority controlling of the undertaking's issued shares, or, finally, in the form of the right to appoint the majority of the undertaking's management board. Under the GATT Agreement on Government Procurement, the term 'public authorities' is confined to central governments and their agencies only.

Public contracts

Public supplies contracts are contracts for pecuniary consideration concluded in writing between a supplier (natural or legal persons) and public authorities, which include the state, local and regional authorities and bodies governed by public law, having as their objective the purchase and delivery of goods.

Public works contracts are contracts for pecuniary consideration concluded in writing between a contractor (natural or legal persons) and public authorities, which include the state, local and regional authorities and bodies governed by public law, having as their objective the completion of works / construction projects.

Public services contracts are contracts for pecuniary consideration concluded in writing between a service provider (natural or legal persons) and public authorities, which include the state, local and regional authorities and bodies governed by public law, having as their objective the provision of services, as defined in the United Nations Product and Service Classification nomenclature.

Public contracts in the utilities sector embrace supplies and works contracts between natural or legal persons and entities operating in transport, water, energy and telecommunications sectors.

Specific types of contracts under the public procurement directives

Concession contracts

A public works concession is defined by the works directive as a written contract between a contractor and a contracting authority concerning either the execution or both the execution and design of a work and for which the consideration consists at least partly in the right to exploit the construction. As will be explained below, the directive contains a mitigated regime with respect to public works concession contracts, which only have to comply with the common rules on advertising.

Subsidized works contracts

Works contracts which are subsidized directly by more than 50 per cent by the state, can still fall within the scope of the directive. Works which are not subsidized directly, or which are subsidized for less than 50 per cent, fall outside this anti-circumvention provision. Not all subsidized works fall within the scope of the directive: only civil engineering works, such as the construction of roads, bridges and railways, as well as building work for hospitals, facilities intended for sports, recreation and leisure and university buildings and buildings used for administrative purposes are referred to as subsidized works contracts. This list is exhaustive.

Framework agreements

The utilities directives have introduced a new selection and tendering procedure, namely framework agreements, which is influenced to a large extent by the benefits of chain supply management and partnership schemes. The supplies, works and services directives do not refer to framework agreements. A framework agreement is an agreement between a contracting authority and one or more suppliers, contractors or service-providers, the purpose of which is to establish the terms, in particular with regard to prices and, where appropriate, the quantity envisaged, governing the contracts to be awarded during a given period. A framework agreement does not posses binding character and should not be considered as a contract between the relevant parties.[1] In practical terms it represents a sort of a standing offer which remains valid during its time-span. Within the provisions of the utilities directive, when a contracting authority awards a framework agreement under the relevant procedures which are common to other public contracts covered therein, subsequent individual contracts concluded under the framework agreement may be awarded without having recourse to a call for competition. Individual contracts which have been awarded under a framework agreement are subject to the requirement of the publication of a contract-award notice in the *Official Journal*. The directive specifically stipulates that misuse of framework agreements may distort competition and trigger the application of the relevant rules, particularly with reference to concerted practices which lead to collusive tendering.

1. Framework agreements should not be confused with framework contracts, the latter producing binding effects; see P.Armin-Trepte, 'Public Procurement in the EC', *CCH Europe*, 1993 p. 93.

In-house contracts and contracts to affiliated undertakings

Article 6 of the services directive provide for the inapplicability of the directive to service contracts which are awarded to an entity which is itself a contracting authority within the meaning of the directive on the basis of an exclusive right which is granted to the contracting authority by a law, regulation or administrative provision of the member state in question.[2] Article 13 of the utilities directive provides for the exclusion of certain contracts between contracting authorities and affiliated undertakings. An affiliated undertaking, for the purposes of Article 1(3) of the utilities directive, is one the annual accounts of which are consolidated with those of the contracting entity in accordance with the requirements of the seventh company law directive (Council Directive 83/349 (OJ 1983 L193/1)). These are service contracts which are awarded to a service-provider which is affiliated to the contracting entity, and service contracts which are awarded to a service-provider which is affiliated to a contracting entity participating in a joint venture formed for the purpose of carrying out an activity covered by the directive. The explanatory memorandum accompanying the text amending the utilities directive (COM (91) 347-SYN 36 1) states that this provision relates, in particular, to three types of service provision within groups. These categories, which may not or may not be distinct, are: the provision of common services such as accounting, recruitment and management; the provision of specialized services embodying the know-how of the group; and the provision of a specialized service to a joint venture. The exclusion from the provisions of the directive is subject, however, to two conditions: the service-provider must be an undertaking affiliated to the contracting authority, and at least 80 per cent of its average turnover arising within the European Community for the preceding three years must derive from the provision of the same or similar services to undertakings with which it is affiliated. The Commission is empowered to monitor the application of this article and to require the notification of the names of the undertakings concerned and the nature and value of the service contracts involved.

2. This practice resembles the market-testing process often employed in the United Kingdom between a contracting authority and an in-house team; see I. Harden, 'Defining the range of application of the public sector procurement directives in the United Kingdom', *Public Procurement Law Review*, 1992, Vol.1 p.362.

Secret public works contracts

The works directive does not apply to works contracts which are declared secret, or the execution of which must be accompanied by special security measures in accordance with the laws, regulations or administrative provisions in force in the member state concerned; nor does the directive apply to works contracts when the protection of the basic interests of the member state's security so requires.

Construction projects under international agreements

The works directive does not apply to public works contracts awarded in pursuance of certain international agreements; nor does the directive apply to public works contracts awarded pursuant to the particular procedure of an international organization. Several international organizations, such as NATO, have their own rules on the award of public works contracts.

Size of public contracts under the public procurement directives

Thresholds

The European rules of public procurement and all the requirements laid down in them are triggered only if certain value thresholds are met. The thresholds laid down are as follows:

- ECU 5 m. for all work and construction projects.
- ECU 200,000 for supplies contracts within the European Union and ECU 136,000 for supplies contracts from third countries which participate in the GATT Agreement on Government Procurement (USA, Canada, Japan, Singapore, Hong Kong, Norway, Switzerland and Israel).
- ECU 600,000 for supplies of telecommunication equipment, under the utilities directive, and ECU 400,000 for all other supplies contracts awarded by public utilities.
- ECU 200,000 for services contracts.

Estimation of contract value

The way in which the value of a contract is calculated is crucial for the application of the relevant directive. To ensure that identical calculation methods are used throughout the European Community and to prevent intentional avoidance of the procurement directives by artificially low contract valuations, the directives lay down specific rules.

Where the contract is to be concluded in the form of a lease, rental or hire-purchase agreement, the calculation, method varies according to the contract's duration. The estimated value is to be calculated on the basis of:

- where its term is twelve months or less, the total value for the contract's duration;
- where its term exceeds twelve months, the total value for the contract's duration, including the estimated residual value of the products;
- where the contract is concluded for an indefinite period, or where its term cannot be defined, the monthly value multiplied by 48;
- where contracts are of a regular nature or are to be renewed over a given period, the following must be taken into account:

  either the actual aggregate value of similar successive contracts awarded over the previous twelve months or accounting period, adjusted where possible for anticipated changes in quantity or value over the subsequent twelve months;
  or the estimated aggregate value of the successive contracts concluded during the twelve months following the initial delivery or accounting periods, where this exceeds twelve months.

  In any event, the choice between these two valuation methods must not be made with the intention of keeping contracts outside the scope of the directive.

If a proposed procurement of supplies of the same type may lead to contracts being awarded at the same time in separate lots, the estimated value of all the lots must be taken into account. If it reaches the relevant threshold, all the lots must be awarded in compliance with the directive. The same rules apply when estimating the value of leasing, rental or hire-purchase contracts. Where provision is explicitly made for options, the basis for calculating the estimated contract value must be the highest possible total permitted for the purchase, lease, rental or hire options included.

When calculating the value of a public works contract, account has to be taken of the estimated value of the works and of the estimated value of the supplies needed to carry out the works, even if these supplies are made available to the contractor by the contracting authorities.

The estimated value of work which the contracting authority intends to have carried out later by the contractor awarded the current contract, and which consists in a repetition of the work to be carried out under the current contract, must be included in the contract value.

The works directive provides for special rules when a contract is subdivided into several lots. When the aggregate value of the lots is over ECU 5m., the provisions of the directive apply to all lots. A work or a contract may not be split up with the intention of avoiding the applicability of the directive. However, lots of a value net of VAT less than ECU 1 m. may be exempted from the scope of the directive, provided that the total estimated value of all the lots exempted does not exceed 20 per cent of the total estimated value of all lots.

The principles of the directives

Mandatory advertisment and publication of public contracts

One of the most important principles of the public procurement directives is the principle of transparency. Transparency is achieved through Community-wide publicity of public procurement contracts over the relevant thresholds by means of publication of three kinds of notice in the *Official Journal* of the European Communities:

(1) Periodic indicative notices (PIN): every contracting entity must notify its intentions for public procurement contracts within the forthcoming financial year.
(2) Invitations to tender: all contracts above the relevant thresholds should be tendered and the notice containing the

invitation to tender must include the award procedures and the award criteria for the contract in question.

(3) Contract award notices (CAN): this is a form of notification after the award of the contract of the successful tenderer and the price of its offer, as well as the reasons for its selection by the contracting authority.

Notices are published by the Publications Office of the European Communities. Within twelve days (or five days, in the case of the accelerated form of restricted or negotiated procedures), the Publications Office publishes the notices in the Supplement to the *Official Journal* and via the TED (Tenders Electronic Daily) database. Two notices are published in full in their original language only and in summary form in the other Community languages. The Publications Office takes responsibility for the necessary translations and summaries. The cost of publishing notices in the Supplement to the *Official Journal* are borne by the Community.

Selection and qualification criteria

Selection criteria are determined through two major categories of qualification requirements; legal, and technical/economic. Contracting authorities must follow objectively determined and homogeneously specified selection criteria for enterprises participating in the award procedures of public procurement contracts. This would eliminate potential grounds for discrimination on grounds of nationality and in combination with the prohibition of technical specifications which are capable of favouring national undertakings, will eventually help create the required background for the liberalization of the Community's public markets.

Legal requirements

The definition of a contractor wishing to submit a tender for the award of a public contract comprises any legal or natural person involved in supplies, construction or services activities. It also includes private consortia, as well as joint ventures or groupings. Contracting authorities may impose a requirement as to the form and legal status of the contractor that wins the award. This requirement focuses only on the post-selection stage, after the award of the contract and indicates the need for legal certainty. Requiring specific legal form and status by contracting entities facilitates monitoring of the performance of the contract and allows better access to justice in the event of a dispute between the contracting entity and the undertaking in question. The successful contractor should also fulfil certain qualitative requirements concerning his eligibility and technical capacity and his financial and economic standing.

Eligibility requirements

In principle, there are automatic grounds for exclusion when a contractor, supplier or service provider

(1) is bankrupt or is being wound up;
(2) is the subject of proceedings for a declaration of bankruptcy or for an order for compulsory winding up;
(3) has been convicted for an offence concerning his professional conduct;
(4) has been guilty of grave professional misconduct;
(5) has not fulfilled obligations relating to social security contributions;
(6) has not fulfilled obligations relating to the payment of taxes.

Financial and economic standing

Evidence of financial and economic standing may be provided by means of:

(1) appropriate statements from bankers;
(2) the presentation of the firm's balance sheets, or extracts from the balance sheets, where these are published under company law provisions;
(3) a statement of the firm's annual turnover and the turnover on construction works for the three previous financial years.

Technical capacity

The technical knowledge and ability of a contractor

In construction projects, the references which the contractor may be required to produce must be specified in the notice or invitation to tender. They include:

- the contractor's educational and professional qualifications, or those of the firm's managerial staff, and, in particular, those of the person or persons responsible for carrying out the works;
- a list of the works carried out over the past five years, accompanied by certificates of satisfactory execution for the most important works. These certificates shall indicate the value, date and site of the works and shall specify whether they were carried out according to the rules of the trade and properly completed. Where necessary, the competent authority shall submit these certificates direct to the authority awarding the contracts;
- a statement of the tools, plant and technical equipment available to the contractor for carrying out the work;
- a statement of the firm's average annual manpower and number of managerial staff for the last three years;
- a statement specifying the technicians or technical divisions which the contractor can call upon for carrying out the work, whether or not they belong to the firm.

The technical capacity of a supplier

In supplies contracts, the references which may be requested must be mentioned in the invitation to tender, and are the following:

- a list of the principal deliveries effected in the past three years, with the sums, dates and recipients, public or private, involved:
  - — where to public authorities awarding contracts, evidence is to be in the form of certificates issued or countersigned by the competent authority;
  - — where to private purchasers, delivery is to be certified by the purchaser or, failing this, simply declared to have been effected by the supplier;
- a description of the undertaking's technical facilities, its measures for ensuring quality and its study and research facilities;
- an indication of the technicians or technical bodies involved, whether or not belonging directly to the undertaking, especially those responsible for quality control;
- samples, descriptions or photographs of the products to be supplied, the authenticity of which must be certified if the contracting authority so requests;

- certificates drawn up by official quality-control institutes or agencies of recognized competence attesting conformity to certain specifications or standards of goods clearly identified by references to specifications or standards;
- where the goods to be supplied are complex or, exceptionally, are required for a special purpose, a check carried out by the contracting authorities (or on their behalf by a competent official body of the country in which the supplier is established, subject to that body's agreement) on the production capacities of the supplier and, if necessary, on his study and research facilities and quality control measures.

List of recognized contractors

Registration in lists of recognized contractors that exist in various member states may be used by contractors as an alternative means of proving their suitability, even to contracting authorities of other member states. Information deduced from registration in an official list may not be questioned by contracting authorities. Nonetheless, the actual level of financial and economic standing and technical knowledge or ability required of contractors is determined by the contracting authorities. Consequently, contracting authorities are required to accept that a contractor's financial and economic standing and technical knowledge and ability are sufficient for works corresponding to his classification only in so far as that classification is based on equivalent criteria with respect to the capacities required.

The award of public contracts

Tendering procedures

Participation in tendering procedures may be through open, negotiated or restricted procedures.

- Open procedures are those where every interested supplier, contractor or service provider may submit an offer.
- Negotiated procedures are such procedures for the award of public contracts whereby contracting authorities consult contractors of their choice and negotiate the terms of the contract with one or more of them. In most cases they follow

restricted procedures and they are heavily utilized under framework agreements in the utilities sectors. There are two different kinds of negotiated procedures: negotiated procedures with prior notification, and negotiated procedures without prior notification.

— Negotiated procedures with prior notification provide for selection of candidates in two rounds. In the first round, all interested contractors may submit their tenders and the contracting authority selects, from the candidates, those who will be invited to negotiate. In the second round, negotiations with various candidates take place and the successful tender is selected. In principle, the minimum number of candidates to be selected is three, provided that there is a sufficient number of suitable candidates.

— Negotiated procedures without prior notification are the least restrictive of the various award procedures laid down in the directive and may be conducted in one single round. Contracting authorities are allowed to choose whichever contractor they want, begin negotiations directly with this contractor and award the contract to him. The directive provides for only a few rules with which this procedure must comply. A prior notice in the *Official Journal* is not required.

- Finally, restricted procedures for the award of public contracts are those whereby only certain contractors invited by the contracting authority may submit tenders. The selection of the winning tender takes place in two rounds. In the first round, all interested contractors may submit their tenders and the contracting authority selects, from the candidates, those who will be invited to tender. In principle, the minimum number of candidates to be selected is five. In the second round, bids are submitted and the successful tender is selected.

An accelerated form of restricted or negotiated procedure may be used where, for reasons of urgency, the periods normally required under the normal procedures cannot apply. In such cases, contracting authorities are required to indicate in the tender notice published in the *Official Journal* the grounds for using the accelerated form of the procedure. The use of an accelerated procedure must be limited to the types and quantities of products or services which it can be shown are urgently required. Other products or services must be supplied or provided under open or restricted procedures.

The directives stipulate that open procedures, where possible, should be the norm. Open procedures increase competition without doubt and can achieve better prices for the contracting authorities when purchasing goods in large volumes. Price reduction based on economies of scale can bring about substantial cost savings for the public sector. Open procedures are mostly utilized when the procurement process is relatively straightforward, and are combined with the lowest price award criterion. Competition in tendering procedures is limited by using the restricted and negotiated procedures. By definition, the number of candidates that are allowed to tender is limited (five in restricted three in negotiated procedures), therefore the directives have attached a number of conditions to be met by the contracting authorities to justify awarding contracts through restricted or negotiated procedures. Restricted and negotiated procedures are utilized in conjunction with the most economically advantageous offer award criterion and are suited for more complex procurement schemes.

Although contracting authorities can freely opt for open or restricted procedures, the latter should be justified by reference to the nature of the products or services to be procured and the balance between contract value and administrative costs associated with tender evaluation. A more rigorous set of conditions apply for the use of negotiated procedures. When negotiated procedures with prior notification are used, they must be justified on grounds of irregular or unacceptable tenders received as a result of a previous call. Negotiated procedures without prior notification are restrictively permitted in the absence of tenders:

- when the procurement involves manufactured products or construction works purely for research and development;
- when for technical or artistic reasons or reasons connected with the protection of exclusive rights a particular supplier or contractor is selected;
- in cases of extreme urgency brought about by unforeseeable events not attributable to the contracting authorities;
- and when additional deliveries and supplies or works would cause disproportionate technical operational and maintenance difficulties.

Prohibition of post-tender negotiations

All negotiations with candidates or tenderers on fundamental aspects of contracts, in particular concerning price, are prohibited in open and restricted procedures; discussions with candidates or tenderers may be held, but only for the purpose of clarifying or supplementing the content of their tenders or the requirements of the contracting authorities, and provided this does not involve discriminatory practices. The need for such a prohibition is clear, since the possibility to negotiate may allow the contracting authority to introduce subjective appraisal criteria.

Tendering procedures for concession contracts

The works directive has adopted a special, mitigated regime for the award of concession contracts. The provisions of the directive only apply to concession contracts whose value is at least ECU 5m. No rules are stipulated as to the way in which the contract value must be calculated.

Design contests

Where the services directive is really novel is in article 1 (g), where provision is made for a fourth type of award procedure, namely design contests, with reference to planning projects. According to article 1 (g), design contests are those national procedures in the fields of area planning, town planning, architecture and civil engineering which enable the contracting authority to acquire a plan or a design selected by a jury, after being put out to competition with or without the award of prizes. The services directive sets out specific rules. The admission of participants to a design contest shall not be limited either by reference to the territory or part of a member state, or on the grounds that under the law of the member state in which the contest is organized, participants would be required to be either natural or legal persons. Furthermore, where design contests are restricted to a limited number of participants, the contracting authorities must lay down clear and non-discriminatory selection criteria which ensure sufficient and genuine competition among the participants. The jury shall be composed exclusively of natural persons who are independent.

Award criteria

In principle, two criteria are laid down in the public procurement directives for awarding public contracts:

- the lowest price;
- the economically most advantageous offer.

The lowest price criterion is self-explanatory. The tenderer who submits the cheapest offer must be awarded the contract. Subject to the qualitative criteria and financial and economic standing, contracting authorities should rely on no other factor than the price quoted to complete the contract. The reasons for utilizing the lowest price criterion are: simplicity, speed and less qualitative consideration during the evaluation of tenders.

The decision as to what is the most economically advantageous tender offer is to be made on a series of factors and determinants chosen by the contracting entity for the particular contract in question. These factors include: price, delivery or completion date, running costs, cost-effectiveness, profitability, technical merit, product or work quality, aesthetic and functional characteristics, after-sales service and technical assistance, commitments with regards to spare parts and components, maintenance costs, and security of supplies.

The award of concession contracts

For the award of concession contracts, contracting authorities must apply similar rules on advertising as apply to open and restricted procedures for the award of every works contract. The provisions on technical standards and on criteria for qualitative selection of candidates and tenderers also apply to the award of concession contracts. The directive does not prescribe the use of specific award procedures for concession contracts, although it presupposes the concession contracts are awarded in two rounds, such as in the case of restricted procedures or negotiated procedures for works contracts. Nothing, however, prevents contracting authorities from applying a single-round open procedure. The directive contains no rules on the minimum number of candidates to be invited to negotiate or to submit a tender. It would seem that a contracting authority may limit itself to selecting only a single candidate, provided the intention to award a concession contract has been adequately published. Under no circumstances may a contracting authority refrain from publishing a notice.

Additional award criteria

Subcontracting and public procurement

Subcontracting plays a major role in the opening up of public markets, as it is the most effective way for small- and medium-sized enterprises to participate in public procurement. All directives on public procurement, influenced by the Commission's Communications on subcontracting and small- and medium-sized enterprises encourage the use of subcontracting in the award of public contracts. Particularly in public supplies contracts, the contracting entity in the invitation to tender may question tenderers on their intentions to subcontract part of the contract to third parties. This reveals the importance of subcontracting for regional development in public procurement. In public works contracts, contracting au thorities awarding the principal contract to a concessionaire may require the concessionaire to subcontract to third parties at least 30 per cent of the total work provided for by the principal contract.

Local labour employment and public procurement

Contracting authorities often are posed with a dilemma concerning the utilization of public procurement contracts, particularly in construction, as a tool for combating long- term unemployment within their region. At first instance, local labour clauses would appear to fall foul of the relevant Treaty provisions on non-discrimination (Article 7) and right of establishment (Article 52). However, the European Court of Justice, in an apparently important case[3] on public procurement, pronounced that the utilization of local labour clauses could be included in the non-exhaustive list of factors determining award criteria, especially the most economically advantageous offer, if they did not have discriminatory effects. The court apparently rejected the possible utilization of local labour clauses as a selection criterion, a decision which is consistent with previous case law, recognizing

3. Case 31/87, *Gebroeders Beentjes BV v. State of Netherlands* [1988] ECR 4635.

the exhaustive character of selection criteria stipulated by the public procurement directives.

Public housing schemes

The award of public housing contracts may deviate from the normal regime of the directive for the purpose of selecting a contractor who meets the requirements specified by the public authority. The scale of work involved in the design and construction of a public housing scheme – the size and complexity of the project, as well as the estimated duration of the work involved – require that planning be based from the outset on close collaboration within a team comprising representatives of the contracting authorities, experts and the contractor to be responsible for carrying out the works. In these cases, the contracting authorities have to apply the advertising rules and the criteria for qualitative selection relating to the restricted procedure. Moreover, the contracting authorities have to include in the contract notice as accurately as possible, a description of the works to be carried out. With respect to quantitative selection, no restrictions apply. Hence, there is no obligation for the contracting authorities to select more that one single contractor to negotiate admission to the building team.

Extraterritorial effects of the public procurement regime

The procurement legal regime of the European Union has been extended in order to cover signatories to the GATT Agreement on Government Procurement.[4] Foreign (third country) firms can participate in tendering procedures for the award of public contracts from public entities in the Common Market, and vice-versa – European firms can participate in tendering procedures in foreign public markets. The GATT Agreement on Government Procurement embraces the following countries: USA, Canada, Japan, the EFTA countries, Singapore, Hong Kong and Israel, and promises considerable improvement in reciprocal market access.

4. See EC Council Regulation 1461/93 (OJ 1993, L146) and EC Council Decision 93/324 (OJ 1993, L125).

The first public procurement directives were inapplicable to products originating in and supplied by third countries. In practical terms the meaning of this limitation was that, in order to be subject to a public contract regulated by one of the directives, a product from outside the Community had to be lawfully put in free circulation in at least one member state. The Council, conscious of the above limitation, adopted a Resolution concerning access to Community public supply contracts for products originating in non-member states. At the same time, negotiations in the international framework were being carried under the GATT Tokyo Round (1973–79). Finally, on 12 April 1979, the GATT Agreement on Government Procurement (AGP) was concluded and became part of the Community's legal structure by virtue of Article 228(2) EECT and Council Decision 80/271.

The agreement on government procurement

The primary aims of the AGP were similar to those of Supplies Directive 77/62: transparency of laws and procedures on government procurement, and elimination of protection for domestic suppliers and discrimination between foreigner suppliers.[5] However, the AGP provisions went further than those of Directive 77/62, by introducing more favourable conditions for tenders from outside the Community; the AGP was envisaged as the vehicle for establishing an international framework of rights and obligations with respect to government procurement, with a view to achieving liberalization and expansion of world trade. As a consequence, third countries-signatories to the AGP are under an obligation to provide for the same opportunities for access to Community tenderers in their respective public markets as those provided for by EC member states to undertakings from these countries. Due to the above modifications, Directive 77/62 was amended. The result of this amendment is that the AGP rules are now incorporated in the supplies regime, which is the only regime in the public procurement sector the application of which produces extraterritorial effects.

The situation under the AGP (Tokyo Round) rules, which have been incorporated in Directive 88/295, is the following: foreign

5. See F.Weiss, 'Public Procurement in the EEC – Public Supply Contracts', *European Law Review*, 1988.

undertakings (from third countries) which have subsidiaries within the Common Market will have the same access to public supplies contracts as European undertakings, and can invoke and enforce Community law both at Community and (mainly) at national level. Obviously, it is required that undertakings from outside the Community must have an economic presence within it. Subsidiaries should take the form of a corporate personality subject to tax laws of the member state within which they operate. It should also be noted that under all public procurement directives, contracting authorities have the right to impose an obligation on one or more undertakings awarded a contract, that the latter take a specific legal form. Suppliers, signatories to the GATT, but not established in the Community, will still be subject to the GATT Agreement on Government Procurement, although they cannot invoke and enforce Community law. They cannot even enforce GATT rules, unless the competent forum (EC member state or third-country GATT signatory) provides for the appropriate remedies. The AGP lays down a rather inoffensive dispute settlement and enforcement procedure, where consultation and conciliation between the aggrieved contractor and the contracting authority play the dominant role. With respect to enforcement of the AGP rules, the Committee on Government Procurement (composed of representatives from each of the parties), as the body responsible for consultation on matters relating to the operation of the AGP or the furtherance of its objectives, has the right to authorize any measure adopted by a party aiming at suspending the reciprocity principle, between that party and another which refuses access to public markets for undertakings of the former. State retreat represents a very interesting compliance method of international trade, which, however, may result in unsatisfactory consequences, as it represents a complex interrelation of private and public law rights. Undertakings which are non-signatories to GATT may face trade restrictions by member states according to Article 115 EECT, which governs the Community's common external policy.

Despite its promising aims and purposes,[6] the AGP-EC regime on public supplies contracts has had a rather limited application as (i) it embraced only its signatories, (ii) it covers only the supply of

6. See the FIDE Congress on Application in the Member States of the Directives on public procurement, Madrid 1990.

products and services that are incidental to the supply contract and not services contracts *per se*, and (iii) it applied only to centrally controlled authorities – local or regional authorities are outside its scope.

The above-mentioned regime has left large areas of procurement activity unregulated by the GATT or by EC secondary legislation. Works and utilities contracts and supply of services have been excluded. Both Community and global public procurement markets are very promising business fields. The Council in its 1977 Resolution noted that the opening up of the public procurement market in respect of non-Community countries could only be accomplished through reciprocity in treatment and mutual balance of advantages. The reciprocity doctrine, or the 'mirror principle', requires that non-member states provide in their domestic markets similar opportunities to those provided by the European member states to undertakings coming from those countries. This means that the element of reciprocity should apply between all European member states and the third country in question. This is a rather unlikely situation, so the Commission in its statement in 1977 concerning Article 115 EECT was prepared to permit a limited and controlled use of it by individual member states, which have established economic and commercial relations with non-member countries in the field of public procurement. During the Tokyo Round negotiations, the Council noted also that Community undertakings were participating in contracts awarded in third countries. This reveals that reciprocity was a bilateral phenomenon in economic activities between a member state and a third country. At first sight, this appears contradictory with the centralized policy that Community institutions seek to apply in the public procurement sector. In this regard, the Commission stated that, in order to prevent deflection of trade between a member state and a third country, it would authorize the former, under Article 115 EECT, to exclude from public contracts certain products, originating in third countries, which are in free circulation in another member state, where similar arrangements (reciprocity effects) have been made for products imported directly. In other words, it was thought that the use of Article 115 EECT might eliminate the 'free rider' phenomenon and 'protect' the benefits gained through a bilateral trade flow between a member state and a third country. From an economic point of view, this tactic may prevent deflection and diversification of trade, but on the other hand, it creates what is sometimes more serious: non-tariff barriers to intra-Community trade. It is difficult, in the framework of an economic union such as the EC, to strike the balance between a common external tariff and individual commercial policies pursued by one or more member states.

One could question why the AGP did not extend its scope to cover works contracts also. It should be recalled that supplies and works contracts were the only regimes covered by public procurement Community legislation during the GATT Tokyo Round (1979). A possible answer could be that supply of products was the maximum that could be agreed, at least at the first stage in the cumbersome and laborious negotiations between the European Communities and GATT signatories. Unlike the EEC Treaty, GATT does not prohibit discrimination by government purchasing agencies in favour of national products. Under the EC regime, discrimination based on nationality grounds is not justified. National authorities may not justify their discriminatory purchasing practices by invoking concerns for employment and social equity, under the broader goal of promoting greater economic efficiency and industrial adjustment. Under the GATT regime, Article III 8(a) excludes government procurement from the principle of national treatment regarding its regulation. Thus, free movement of goods was considered, with respect to public procurement, to be the first step under the framework of the Multilateral Agreements between the EC and GATT signatories with a view to liberalizing trade and preventing non-tariff barriers arising from national procurement policies.

Another possible justification of the limitation of the AGP rules to supplies of goods only could have been that works and construction contracts involve further aspects that must be taken into account in an attempt to liberalize their regime. They involve social and regional policy, short- and long-term employment considerations, peripheral development of the EC regions, etc. Liberalizing the public works regime between the Community and third countries will not only bring into play free trade area considerations (free movement of goods), but will also go further, trespassing on the field of economic union, where labour, capital, payments and services need also to circulate freely.[7]

7. See L.Gormley, 'Some reflections on Public Procurement in the EEC', *European Business Law Review*, Nov. 1990.

The Utilities Directive 90/531 intends to open up procurement practices in the four previously excluded sectors – water, energy, telecommunications and transport – mainly to EC-wide competition. With regard to goods (and services) originating in third countries, things are more complicated. A product from outside the Community, in order to be subject to a public contract regulated by one of the EC public procurement directives, must lawfully be put in free circulation in at least one member state. Except where there has been an international agreement which grants comparable and effective access for Community undertakings to public markets of a third country (the reciprocity principle), Article 29 of Directive 90/531 renders it possible for EC contracting authorities in the utilities sector to reject offers from outsde the Community and requires Community preference where Community offers are equivalent to offers from third countries (i.e. where the price difference does not exceed 3 per cent). With reference to an international agreement granting access to public markets, Directive 90/531 opens the door for the application of the GATT Agreement on Government Procurement in the utilities sector, concluded between the European Community and eleven GATT signatories during the 1979 GATT Tokyo Round. The AGP embraces only supplies contracts, which are currently the only public sector regime open to international competition. The European Union's commitment to international liberalization of public markets has been demonstrated by its offer to the GATT AGP signatories during the Uruguay Round, to eliminate all discrimination regarding contracts in urban transport, ports, airports, heavy electrical and telecommunications equipment.[8]

Expansion of the AGP framework to embrace supplies and works contracts in the utilities sector and services contracts has being pursued during the GATT Uruguay Round.[9] The new regime introduced substantial changes in the application of the AGP with respect to types of contracts and coverage of contracting authorities as well as remedies. Works and services contracts are now covered and the list of contracting authorities embraces not only central government departments and their agencies but

8. See Council Regulation 1461/93, OJ 1993, L146, on access to public contracts for tenderers from the United States; Council Decision 93/323, OJ 1993, L125, on the conclusion of agreement between the EEC and USA on government procurement.

9. Article XXIV 1 AGP, signed on 15 April, 1994 by all the previous signatories exept Hong Kong and Singapore.

regional and local authorities and some utilities in the form of public authorities or public undertakings. Certain exemptions between the signatories do apply, but based on bilateral agreements, the new regime promises a significant expansion of the existing European procurement legislation.[10]

With respect to the EFTA countries, on 22 October 1991 the EC reached an agreement with the seven states involved (the European Economic Area) to participate in the Single Market from 1 January 1993. This changed the framework under the preferential agreement regime in existence prior to 1991[11] to a free trade area, the EFTA states being required to implement Community law, and of course EC public procurement directives, in their national legal systems. The regime applies also to Hungary and Poland, by virtue of their Association Agreements.[12]

10. The applicability of the new AGP by its signatories is subject to its ratification before 1 January, 1996.
11. See F.Weiss, 'The Law of Public Procurement in EFTA and the EEC; The legal framework and its implementation', *Yearbook of European Law*, 1987.
12. OJ 1993, L347/36 and OJ 1993, L348/36.

CHAPTER FOUR

The impact of public procurement legislation on the demand and the supply sides

A useful instrument for the assessment of the impact of public procurement legislation on the demand and supply sides is the examination of the relevant case law before the competent fora. Such an impact assessment exercise would probably shed light on the persisting obstacles to public sector integration and the liberalization of public markets throughout Europe, which are mainly originated in national administrations, as well as illuminating the response of the industry to such fundamental legislative changes.

Litigation concerning public procurement may take place in two fora: the European Court of Justice and national courts. Two patterns with respect to the impact of public procurement legislation on the demand and supply sides have developed since the enactment of the directives. One pattern relates to the utilization of the ECJ's rulings as a guide for the direct effectiveness and/or the interpretation of provisions of the relevant directives. This pattern has been identified in case law related to Article 177 EECT proceedings. The other pattern is associated with compliance of defaulting member states that failed to implement correctly public procurement directives and has been pursued through the application of Article 169 EECT proceedings. The latter pattern often occurs during the early stages of implementation of public procurement legislation into domestic legal orders and reveals the impact of the new regime on existing national systems, although it is not surprising that well after the completion of the internal market, compliance proceedings are still being brought before the ECJ. The former pattern occurs in cases where clarification and interpretation of provisions of the relevant directives is needed and can be associated with the post-implementation era, where the directives have been digested into the domestic legal orders.

Both patterns reveal the perpetuation by some member states of preferential and discriminatory procurement as the major persisting obstacle to public market integration in the European Community. Failure to comply with the provisions of the relevant directives, as well as incorrect and illegal application of them by contracting authorities, constitute the most important non-tariff barrier in the European integration process. While technical standards and specifications have been harmonized to a considerable degree in order to eliminate any potential ground for discrimination based on nationality, the movement of goods and services related to public markets remains distorted, more so than the movement of good and services destined for private markets. The following analysis of seemingly important case law in the field of public procurement, at both Community and national levels, provides a picture of the response of the players to the legislative changes introduced by European institutions.

Judicial review at European level

The enactment of national legislation or the employment of administrative practices with a view to implementing public procurement directives has been subject to a double regime of judicial control at Community and at national levels. Since the forms and methods of incorporation of secondary Community legislation into national provisions rely mainly on the discretion of member states, the EEC Treaty primarily envisaged a centralized Community judicial control in order to ensure that member states fulfil their obligations. This sort of judicial review includes proceedings under Article s 169, 170, 171 EECT, which include actions against a member state for failure to fulfil Treaty obligations. Under Article 169 EECT, it is the European Commission that brings a member state before the Court of Justice. Other member states may avail themselves of the provisions laid down in Article 170 EECT to bring before the court a member state's infringement of the Treaty. Both proceedings lack an enforcement mechanism and the Court's judgment has only a declaratory character. Even under Article 171 EECT, where the court may continue to condemn a member state's failure to comply with a previous judgment, enforcement proceedings are lacking.

It has been suggested that Community institutions may take sanctions against a member state that has failed to fulfil its obligations under the Treaty and to comply with a court's judgment.[1] There is a parallel under the ECSC Treaty, but in fact, such action has never been taken. Centralized Community judicial control also covers proceedings under Article 177 EECT, where national courts make references to the Court of Justice for preliminary rulings on the interpretation of EC legislation and the compatibility of national laws with the former, but this sort of review lies on the borderline between Community and national jurisdiction. It should be mentioned here that in the area of public procurement, non-compliance with the European directives may lead to the withdrawal of Community funds allocated to the defaulting member state. This appears an effective from of sanction, initiated by the European Commission, after a decision of the ECJ pronouncing on the non-compliance issue.

National courts can claim jurisdiction upon a member state's failure to fulfil Treaty obligations when primary and secondary Community legislation is directly applicable and directly effective. Direct applicability of Community law means that there is no need for implementing measures to be taken by member states, whereas direct effectiveness implies the reliance of individuals upon Community law before national courts.[2] With respect to directives, they are not directly applicable, as member states are required to introduce implementing measures and the direct effectiveness of their provisions depends on three conditions being met, as defined by the Court of Justice: the sufficient clarity and precision of their provisions, their unconditionality and, finally, the lack of discretion on the part of member states when implementing them. Direct effectiveness is closely linked with the normative character of Community law.

Judicial control of member states' obligations arising from public procurement directives is both Community and nationally

1. See Kapteyn and Verloren van Themaat, *Introduction to the law of the European Communities*, 3rd edn, Deventer: Kluwer, 1989, p.35.
2. See the ECJ's judgment in case 26/62 *NV Algemene Transport-en Expeditie Onderneming Van Gend en Loos v. Nederlandse Administrtie der Belastigen* [1963] ECR 1. Also cases 57/65 *Alfons Luttucke GmbH v. Haupzollampt Saarlouis* [1966] ECR 205, and 28/67 *Firma Molkerei Zentrale Westfalen/Lippe GmbH v. Haupzollampt Paderborn*, [1968] ECR 143.

oriented. The Community centralized judicial review has been channelled through proceedings under Article 169 EECT, although it is worth mentioning that the EC Commission has availed itself of the proceedings under Article 185 EECT which referred to interim measures ordered by the ECJ. National judicial control often ends in a reference to the ECJ under Article 177 EECT for a preliminary ruling with respect to the interpretation of the directives' provisions or the compatibility with Communty law of national laws implementing them. It is obvious that, although the public procurement sector is dominated by national sensibilities, thus requiring a decentralized control, Community control plays the dominant role.

The European Commission, by virtue of Article 169 EECT, may initiate proceedings, on its own initiative or in response to a complaint, against a defaulting member state for failure to fulfil its obligations under the Treaty. The existence of specific legal interest is not required[3] as a condition of the admissibility of the action, since it is in the general interest of the Commission to observe, supervise and ensure the correct application of Community law. There have been fifteen cases under Article 169 EECT, the majority of which were attributable to the Italian state's failure to comply with the provisions of public procurement directives. Nine out of the fifteen cases under Article 169 have been brought against Italy; two against Greece and one each against Ireland, Spain, Portugal and Denmark. Interestingly, the ECJ granted interim measures under Article 185 EECT in three cases – one against Ireland and the others against Italy. In all cases, the award of the contract in question was suspended. Examination, in chronological order, of the relevant cases and analysis of the court's judgments should reveal the underlying obstacles to the opening-up of public procurement which are mainly attributable to national administrations.

In 1976 the very first public procurement case[4] was initiated by the EC Commission against Italy for failure to fulfil its obligations under Directive 71/305, particularly failure to provide for implementing measures concerning open procedures, advertising of tenders in the *Official Journal*, implementing qualitative selection criteria, etc. What is interesting in this case is that the Commission recognized that instruments such as Directive 71/305 (and 77/62)

3. Case 167/73 *Commission v.France* [1974] ECR 359.
4. Case 10/76, *Commission v. Italy* [1976] ECR 1359.

aim at circumscribing the extent of the discretionary powers of public authorities; thus the national measures for giving effect to them inevitably should have the nature of legislative acts – mandatory and binding on the administration, and capable of creating rights for individuals enforceable before courts. The fact that other member states do not consider it appropriate to give effect to these provisions by way of legislation, in the eyes of the Commission, does not matter, as long as at the practical level, the substance the directive is applied. The Commission accepted a slightly different position from previous case law of the European Court of Justice, where the latter ruled that administrative practices are not considered appropriate measures for implementing EC directives. The Commission's position represented a flexible approach to the implementation of public procurement directives, as it focuses on the practical operation of the implementing measures, and not on their form.

Four years later, in 1980 the Italian state was again brought before the ECJ.[5] In this case the court condemned the non-implementation of Directive 77/62 into Italian law. It declared that Directive 77/62 was intended to supplement the prohibition on restrictions on the free movement of goods laid down by Article 30 EECT by introducing equal conditions of competition for public supply contacts, in order to ensure a degree of transparency allowing the observance of the prohibition in question to be better supervised. Italy claimed that a number of extraordinary circumstances had prevented the enactment of the law required to incorporate the directive in question into the national legal order. It was the dissolution of the legislature – an extraordinary event, according to the defendant – owing to the fundamental requirements of the democratic system, which temporarily paralysed the legislature functions conferred on Parliament. The court rejected that argument, stating that a member state may not plead provisions, practices or circumstances existing in its internal legal system in order to justify a failure to comply with the obligations imposed by Community directives. This judgment is in accordance with the principle of public international law which lays down that states are not allowed to invoke internal constitutional circumstances in order to avoid international obligations. Moreover, this decision of the court appears to be a

5. Case 133/80, *Commission v. Italy* [1981] ECR 457.

policy one, so as to close the door to member states' attempts to plead internal legal requirements as an excuse for failure to fulfil their obligations under the EEC Treaty.

Italy had to appear again before the Court of Justice in 1983,[6] when it apparently had failed to fulfil its obligations in implementing correctly Directive 71/305. In particular, a provision of Italian Law No.741 (Article 10) added a further criterion (a tender which equals the average tender or is closest to it) to those laid down in article 29 of Directive 71/305, concerning the criteria for the award of a contract. The latter Article seems to contain an exhaustive list of grounds on which a contract may be awarded: either the lowest price tender or the most economically advantageous offer. The former relies purely on quantitative criteria, whereas the latter presupposes a combination of quantitative and qualitative criteria that vary according to the contract in question (price, period of completion, running cost, profitability, technical merit). The defendant claimed to have intended to determine the correct market price by excluding extremely low tenders not corresponding to reality, without having recourse to article 29 of Directive 71/305 (seeking of explanations from the tenderer). The court rejected that argument. Advocate-General Lenz[7] concluded that extremely low tenders may be considered by contracting authorities laying down minimum prices for participation in the competition for the award of a contract, although he admitted that prices may change considerably between an invitation to tender and the completion of the project, due to inflation.

In 1985 the Commission was informed that the Municipality of Milan had awarded a works contract without following the provisions of Directive 71/305 concerning prior publication of a notice for tender in the *Official Journal*. It initiated proceedings against Italy.[8] The Italian state relied on article 9 of Directive 71/305, which stipulates an exception from the common rules in a number of occasions and particularly with respect to the case in question, when exclusive rights held by the undertaking to which the contract was awarded are involved (art.9(b)) or when the project is a matter of extreme urgency due to unforeseeable events (art.9(d)). The court rejected both justifications. As for the

6. Case 247/83, *Commission v. Italy* [1985] ECR 1077.
7. See his Conclusions in [1985] ECR 1084.
8. Case 199/85, *Commission v. Italy* [1987] ECR 1039.

exception laid down in article 9(b), exclusive rights include know-how and intellectual property rights that are necessary to build a plant of the type required. For future relating cases, justification on these grounds brings into play competition law considerations, as Regulation 556/89 on know-how licensing, and Regulation 2349/84 on patent licences agreements must be taken into account. With regard to the grounds provided for in art.9(d), extreme urgency brought by events unforeseen by the authorities must be restrictively interpreted, as it is subject to a justification test based on the proportionality principle.

One year later it was the turn of Greece to appear before the court,[9] where the Commission brought an action under Article 169 EECT procedure seeking the Court to declare the failure of the Greek State to fulfil its obligations under Article 30 EECT and Directive 77/62. The case concerned conditions for the award of public supplies contracts, in particular conditions of access to them. Advocate-General Mischo condemned a circular of the Minister of National Economy (Circular of 11 July 1983) which favoured domestic products in public supplies contracts. The circular imposed a coefficient of 21 per cent on prices of imported products.

In 1987 the Irish Dundalk pipeline case[10] was before the Court of Justice after the Commission had received complaints that Ireland had not complied with Directive 71/305. Although the contract in question concerned the transportation of drinking water, a sector which has been expressly excluded from the framework of Directive 71/305 by virtue of article 3(5), Ireland had requested the publication of the relevant notice in the *Official Journal*, thus voluntarily bringing itself within the scope of the directive. The fact that it made use of the directive's provisions concerning the obligatory publication of contract notices was not enough to counter article 3(5) of Directive 71/305, which excludes its application in contracts relating to water distribution services. The court, on the grounds of legal certainty and legitimate expectation, pronounced on the inadmissibility of the action as far as the infringement of Directive 71/305 was concerned. What is interesting in this case is the Commission's argumentation, supported by Spain acting as an intervener, on article 10 of Directive 71/305. This provision prohibits member states from

9. Case 84/86, *Commission v. Hellenic Republic*, not reported.
10. Case 45/87, *Commission v. Ireland* [1988] ECR 4929.

introducing into the contractual clauses relating to a given contract, technical specifications, unless they are justified by the subject of the contract, which mention products of a specific make or source or a particular process which favour or eliminate certain undertakings. Such indications are only permitted if they are accompanied by the words 'or equivalent' where the authorities awarding contracts are unable to give sufficiently precise and ineligible specifications of the subject of the contract. The Irish invitation to tender contained reference to (Irish) technical specifications which were not justified by the subject of the contract. Several standards other than that imposed by a clause in the tender invitation provided equivalent guarantees of safety, performance and reliability. Were this not the case, the Irish standards would only have been permitted if the words 'or equivalent' had been added. Those words were not in cluded in the relevant clause. The latter, although escaping from the framework of Directive 71/305, fell foul of Article 30 EECT on the grounds that it was liable to impede imports of foreign products (pipes) into Ireland. Invocation of Article 36 and the rule of reason were rejected as unjustified. The President of the Court ordered the suspension of the award of the contract after an application made by the Commission. Finally, the contract was awarded to the contractor in question on condition that the words 'or equivalent' would be included in the tender notice in the *Official Journal*.

In 1988, the ECJ granted interim measures in an application made by the Commission against Italy[11] ordering the latter to suspend the award of a contract or, alternatively, had the contract been awarded, to adopt all the appropriate measures in order to cancel the award or at least to preserve the status quo until the judgment was given. The application for interim measures was very similar to that in the Dundalk case, in particular with respect to the cancellation of the contract had it already been awarded.[12] The court granted the order. It also pronounced that exploratory contracts fall under the meaning of 'contract' in article 1 of Directive 71/305, as it governs the procedure for awarding works contracts whenever they are awarded. 'Exploratory' means that the contracting authority has no direct intention to procure, but only to search the market.

11. Case 194/88R, *Commission v. Italy* [1988] ECR 5647.
12. See the comments about the role of the Commission under the Compliance Directive 89/665, below.

The same year, the Commission brought Italy again before the court in a case[13] that concerned not only public supplies contracts, but also Article s 52 and 59 EECT (right of establishment and freedom to provide services, respectively). The defendant, by virtue of national law, required that only companies in which all or a majority of the share capital was in public ownership were eligible to participate in and compete for the award of supplies contracts required for the establishment of data-processing systems, the design and in some cases the technical management of these systems. The court ruled that this was contrary to Article s 52 and 59 EECT which are based on the principle of equal treatment and prohibit not only overt discrimination on grounds of nationality, but also all covert forms of discrimination, which, by the application of other criteria of differentiation, lead in fact to the same result. With respect to Directive 77/62, the court held that the establishment of a data-processing system of the type provided by the Italian legislation constituted 'products' within the meaning of article 6(1)(h) of Directive 77/95, which may be dissociated from the activities involved in the development of the data-processing system (these are to be considered services). It also rejected the argument that the award of the contract for data-processing fell under article 2(3) of Directive 77/62, which provides for public service activities covered by special or exclusive rights to be awarded to a specific body, regardless of its legal status. The defendant's submission that the supply contracts in question were secret, or that their delivery must be accompanied by special security reasons, thus allowing the contracting authority to derogate from the basic principles of the directive (publication of tender notice (article 4(1)(2)) was rejected. Although the data involved were essential in the fight against crime in areas of taxation, public health and fraud in agricultural matters, observance of confidentiality by the tenderer concerned was not dependent on public ownership. Even if the suppliers of the data-processing system in issue fell under the exception of article 6(1)(e) of Directive 77/62, which provides for additional deliveries from a specific supplier in order for contracting authorities to avoid the purchase of equipment of different technical characteristics, resulting in incompatibility or disproportionate technical difficulties, cannot justify the rule that only companies

13. Case 3/88, *Commission v. Italy* [1989] ECR 4035.

controlled by the state may be awarded such contracts.

In 1989, the Commission initiated proceedings against Portugal[14] and sought to have the ECJ declare that by not publishing in the *Official Journal* a tender notice issued by Aeroportos e Navegação Aerea calling for tenders for the supply and assembly of a telephone exchange at Lisbon airport, the Portuguese Republic had failed to fulfil its obligations under Directives 77/62 and 88/295. The court accepted that Aeroportos is a contracting authority operating transport services. Supplies contracts in this sector have been expressly excluded from the framework of Directive 77/62 and the amending Directive 88/295, by virtue of article 2(2). The Commission lost the case, as it was held inadmissible.

The same year, by an application lodged at the ECJ, the Commission brought an action against Italy[15] for declaration that Italian Law 80/87 laying down special provisions for accelerating the completion of public works was incompatible with Article 59 EECT and Directives 71/305 and 89/440. That law reserved a proportion of public works to subcontractors whose registered offices were in the region where the works were to be carried out. The court ruled that such provision has an actual or potential discriminatory effect on undertakings outside that particular region and other undertakings from other member states, thus being inconsistent with Article 59 EECT. Furthermore, it represents a criterion of selection that is not mentioned in the works directives (articles 23 to 26, Directive 71/305) and in particular does not reflect any of the requirements of an economic or technical nature provided for in articles 25 and 26 of Directive 71/305.

In 1989 the Commission brought Denmark before the Court in a case of major importance[16] for the Danish government, as it concerned the construction of a bridge linking two parts of the country. The tender notice contained a condition that the contract would be awarded to contractors that employed Danish workforce and used domestic materials for the project. Although the Danish government, after the intervention of the Commission, withdrew the relevant clause from the contract documents, the court considered this immaterial as the contract had already been awarded to a particular company on the grounds of such a clause

14. Case 247/89, *Commission v. Portugal* [1991] ECR I 3659.
15. Case 360/89, *Commission v. Italy* [1992] I ECR 3401.
16. Case 243/89, *Commission v. Denmark*, judgment of 22 June, 1993.

as an award criterion. The Court of Justice condemned Denmark for not complying with the works directive.

Also in 1989 the Commission initiated proceedings for the second time against Greece[17] in a case in which the latter had failed to implement the supplies directives by virtue of administrative circulars. These circulars contained conditions imposing obstacles to access in public supplies markets through quotas reserved to domestic suppliers.

In 1990 Italy was again brought to Luxembourg for two cases. The first[18] concerned an application lodged by the Commission, and a declaration by the ECJ was sought that Italy had failed to fulfil its obligations under Directives 77/62 and 88/295. The Unita Sanitaria Locale XI Genoa (a local health authority) had stipulated that, in order for tenderers to participate in a public supply contract, 50 per cent of the minimum amount of supplies required to have been made over the preceding three years should have been made to public administration authorities. Although such a condition is absolutely inconsistent with the supplies directives, the court did not proceed on the substance of the case and declared the action inadmissible, as the Commission had not observed the proceedings laid down in Article 169 EECT.

The second case[19] concerned an action brought by the Commission under Article 169 in order for the court to declare that Italy had failed to fulfil its obligations under Article 59 EECT (freedom to provide services) and the procurement directives. The invitation for tender made by the Ente Ferrorie delo Stato (Italian State railways) for construction work on a rapid rail line between Rome and Naples included a requirement of a minimum turnover for works carried out in Italy and membership of a national construction industry association. It will be interesting to see if the court will apply the utilities or the works directives in this case.[20]

In 1991 the Commission lodged an application before the ECJ[21] for a declaration that, by failing to communicate for publication in the *Official Journal* an indicative notice summarizing all the contracts which the Italian Ministry of Finance planned to award during that year, and then by failing to publish a notice inviting

17. Case 299/89, *Commission v. Hellenic Republic*, not reported.
18. Case 362/90, *Commission v. Italy* judgment of March 31, 1992.
19. Case 95/90, *Commission v. Italian Republic*, not reported.
20. See the 'Aeroportos' case, 247/89, *loc. cit.* n. 14 above.
21. 272/91R, *Commission v. Italian Republic*, order of 12 June, 1992.

tenders for the concession of the system for the computerization of the lottery, and also by restricting participation in the tendering procedure to bodies, companies, consortia or groups whose capital, individually or collectively, was mainly publicly owned, the Italian government had failed to fulfil its obligations under Articles 30, 52 and 59 EECT and under the Supplies Directives 77/62 and 88/295. The Commission also requested the court to grant interim measures against the Italian state to take all the required measures to suspend either the award of the contract or the cancellation of any contract which might be concluded at a later stage. The Commission claimed that in so far as the tendering procedure was restricted to companies or bodies whose capital was mainly in public ownership, it operated in favour of Italian undertakings and infringed Article 30 EECT; it also constituted a measure having equivalent effect to quantitative restrictions on imports, thus infringing Article 30 EECT. A linkage was sought with case 3/88 *Commission v. Italy,*[22] where the court had held that Italian provisions restricting the conclusion of contracts for the development of data-processing systems for public authorities to companies whose shares were mainly in public ownership were contrary to Articles 52 and 59 EECT. The court observed that the introduction of the computerized system would not alter the operation of the lottery game and the successful tenderer would not be responsible for such operation. The supply of the computerized system resembled development of the data-processing system in case 3/88, but the situation was not clear and as the contract had already been awarded, the court ordered the suspension of the act (Decree of the Minister of Finance) awarding the concession of the system for the computerization of the lottery and the suspension of the contract itself concluded with a consortium.

In 1991 the Commission was successful in an action against Spain[23] where the ECJ declared that Spain had failed to fulfil its obligations under Directive 71/305, in consequence of the decision of the governing council of the Universidad Complutense Madrid to award contracts for works connected with the extension and renovation of the Faculty of Political Science and Sociology and the School of Social Works by private contract (without

22. [1989] ECR 4035.
23. Case 24/91, *Commission v. Kingdom of Spain* [1994] CMLR 621.

publication in the *Official Journal*), which could not be justified under the exception for reasons of urgency unforeseen to the contracting authorities.

In 1992 Italy was once more brought before the ECJ[24] for failure to fulfil obligations under Directive 71/305 as amended by Directive 89/440, in particular to publish in the *Official Journal* the tender notice in respect of the construction of an avalanche barrier in the district of Colle Isarco/Brennero. The case concerned the application of the award procedures by contracting authorities, particularly the negotiated procedures without prior notice. The Italian state contested the Commissions submissions that the public authority in question had awarded the construction works by virtue of a private contracts on the grounds of extreme urgency and unforeseeability, as provided for in article 9 of the works directive. The court, although it recognized the fulfilment urgency criterion, pronounced that the latter must be in a causal link with unforeseeable events (article 9(d)) to contracting authorities in order to deviate from the main provisions of the directive.

In 1992 the Commission sought a declaration from the ECJ[25] concerning Italy's failure to observe Directive 71/305 with respect to publication of an invitation to tender for highway construction between Ascoli and Mare. The contract was awarded privately on the grounds of technical reasons, within the meaning of article 9(b) of the works directive. The court did not had the chance to proceed to the substance of the case, as the Commission's application was held inadmissible due to inconsistencies between its reasoned opinion and its application before the court.

In 1992 Spain had to appear before the ECJ[26] following an action for failure to observe Directives 71/305 and 77/62 brought by the Commission. Spain had maintained in force certain provisions which constituted an exclusion from the application of public procurement rules, provisions allowing contracts to be concluded directly without competitive tendering, provisions governing participation and selection criteria and technical standards and finally provisions relating to award criteria. The court declared the incompatibility of the Spanish national laws which implemented the above directives with Articles 30 and 59 EECT and Directives 71/305 and 77/62 themselves.

24. Case 107/92, *Commission v. Italy*, judgment of 2 August, 1993.
25. Case 296/92, *Commission v. Italy*, judgment of 12 January, 1994.
26. Case 71/92, *Commission v. Spain*, judgment of 17 November, 1993.

The same year the Commission brought an action under Article 169 EECT against Spain[27] for failure to comply with Directive 77/62. This action followed up a preliminary ruling reference to the ECJ by a Spanish court on litigation concerning procurement of pharmaceutical products by public authorities. The national litigation related to a framework agreement entered into by Spanish public authorities and the national association of pharmaceutical companies (Farmaindustria), in which the prices and other terms and conditions governing the direct purchase of pharmaceutical products destined for social security institutions and the indirect purchase of such products were laid down. Although the national litigation (*Farmaindustria v. Consejeria de salud de la Junta de Andalucia*)[28] was withdrawn, the Commission proceeded in launching an action against Spain for failure to comply with the provisions of Directive 77/62, on the basis of the incompatibility of the framework agreement with the principles and provisions of that directive.

Judicial review at national level

Individuals may avail themselves of legal remedies before national courts, relying on provisions of Community law armed with direct effectiveness. With respect to public procurement directives, actions against the state, local government and general contracting authorities may be launched on condition that their provisions produce vertical direct effect. Verticality of direct effectiveness implies the responsibility of the state, as a subject of Community law, to individuals as far as the fulfilment of the former's obligations under the Treaty is concerned. On the other hand, horizontal direct effectiveness allows individuals to rely on Community law in actions against other individuals.[29] Interestingly the court rejected the argument that directives may produce horizontal direct effect,[30] on the grounds that their binding nature

27. Case 32/92, *Commission v. Spain* [1994] I ECR 1569.
28. Case 179/89, *Farmaindustria v. Consejeria de salud de la Junta de Andalucia*, [1989] OJ C160/10.
29. The concept of horizontal direct effect has been defined by the Court of Justice in case 13/61 *Kledingverkoopbedrijf de Geus en Uitdenbogerd v.Robert Bosch GmbH*, [1962] ECR 45.
30. Case 152/84 *Marshal v.Southampton and South West Hampshire Area Health Authority*, [1986] ECR 723.

exists only in relation to the member states to which they are addressed.

With respect to public procurement cases subject to domestic litigation, these are based on the doctrine of vertical direct effectiveness of directives' provisions. Individuals may claim the existence of the latter, requesting the court to apply the provision of the directive in question directly, irrespective of any implementing measure adopted by the state. In almost all cases, even if the case is obviously clear or the principle at stake has already been covered by a court's previous materially identical reference,[31] national courts feel safer to ask the Court of Justice for a reference regarding the direct effect of the relevant provision. There have been nine cases before national courts relying on provisions contained in public procurement directives, which have been referred to the ECJ for a preliminary ruling under Article 177 EECT. In five other cases before national courts,[32] the latter dealt with them without having recourse to Article 177 proceedings.

The definition of a contractor wishing to submit a tender for the award of a public contract comprises any legal or natural person involved in supplies, construction or services activities. It also includes private consortia, as well as joint ventures or groupings. With respect to legal qualification criteria, contracting authorities may impose a requirement as to the form and legal status of the contractor that wins the award. This requirement focuses only on the post-selection stage, after the award of the contract, and indicates the need for legal certainty. Specific legal form and status required by contracting entities facilitates monitoring of the performance of the contract and allows better access to justice in the event of a dispute between the contracting entity and the undertaking in question. The successful contractor should also fulfil certain qualitative standards concerning his eligibility and technical capacity and his financial and economic standing, and should submit either the lowest offer or the most economically advantageous one through an open, restricted or negotiated procedure. The majority of litigation initiated before national

31. Case 283/81, *Srl CILFIT v. Ministry of Health*, [1982] ECR 3415. The theories of *acte eclaire* and *acte claire*.

32. Case No.10475 *SA.SHV Belgium v. La Maison Idéale et Société Nationale du Longement*; judgment of 24/6/86 of the Belgian Conseil d'Etat; case 194/84 *P.Steinhauser v.Ville de Biaritz*, before the Tribunal Administratif du Pau; judgment of 24 December 1987 before the District Court of Maastricht and, finally, an arbitration award of the Raad van Arbitrage of 31 March 1987.

courts and later referred to the European Court of Justice focus on the application of selection and award criteria defined in the public procurement directives. Examination of the relevant case law in chronological order prior to the completion of the internal market reveals the problems faced by the supply side.

In case 76/81,[33] a reference for a preliminary ruling from the Conseil d'Etat of the Grand Duchy of Luxembourg was made to the Court. An establishment permit imposed by national legislation (Reglement Grand-Ducal du 6 Novembre 1974) on foreign undertakings seeking to participate in the award of public works and public supplies contracts was held incompatible with the relevant provisions of Directive 71/305 and Article 59 EECT concerning the freedom to provide services. The court held that articles 23 to 26 of Directive 71/305, relating to the criteria of a tenderer's good standing and qualification, are directly effective. These criteria comprise grounds for exclusion from participation in a public contract (article 23), such as bankruptcy, professional misconduct, failure to fulfil social security obligations and obligations relating to taxes. They also refer to technical ability and knowledge of the contractor (article 26), where proof of them may be furnished by educational or professional qualifications, previous experience in performing public contracts and statements on the contractor's expertise. Articles 23 and 26 of the works directive, covering the contractors' eligibility and technical capacity, constitute an exhaustive list. For the purpose of assessing the financial and economic standing of the contractors, article 25 is an exception to the exhaustive list, where contracting entities may request references other than those expressly mentioned therein. Such references include appropriate banker's statements, the presentation of the contractor's balance sheets and an overall turnover statement of the firm.

Official registration in a list in a member state (articles 24 and 28(3)) constitutes a means of proving before the authority of another member state awarding contracts that the tenderer satisfies the qualitative criteria listed in articles 23 to 26 of Directive 71/305. Article 29 of Directive 71/305, which requires the contracting authorities awarding a contract for which an obviously abnormally low tender in relation to the transaction has been submitted, to examine the details of the tender before

33. Case 76/81, *SA Transporoute et Travaux v. Minister of Public Works*, [1982] ECR 457.

deciding the award of the contract, is also directly effective.[34] The contracting authorities are under the duty to seek from the tenderer an explanation of his prices or to inform him that his tender appears to be abnormally low and to allow him a reasonable time within which to submit further details, before making any decision as to the award of the contract. The case did not touch on the concept of 'obviously', abnormally low tenders, which came into play[35] a few years later.

Five years later, in 1986 three joint cases[36] were referred to the European Court of Justice. In these cases the court made the following ruling: article 25 of Directive 71/305 concerning the proof of contractors' economic and financial standing contains a list of references which is non-exhaustive. The value of the works which may be carried out at one time may constitute a proof of contractors' economic and financial standing. The contracting authorities are allowed to fix such a limit, as Directive 71/305 aims not at delimiting the powers of member states, but at determining the references or evidence which may be furnished in order to establish contractors' financial and economic standing. On the other hand, the inclusion of a contractor in an official list of recognized contractors in a member state may be used as an alternative means of proving before the authority of another member state awarding contracts the qualitative criteria listed in articles 23 to 26.[37] However, as harmonization of official lists of recognized contractors (article 28(1)) concerns only the references attesting to financial and economic standing and their technical knowledge and ability, criteria for their classifications are not harmonized. In regard to evidence of contractors' economic and financial good standing, and qualifications, registration in a official list of recognized contractors may replace the references referred to in articles 23 to 26, in so far as such registration is based upon equivalent information. Thus, a request from a contractor recognized in another member state to furnish proof

34. Case No. 10475, *SA SHV Belgium v. La Maison Idéale et Société Nationale du Longement*, before the Belgian Conseil d'Etat.

35. See Case 103/88, *Fratelli Costanzo S.p.A. v. Comune di Milano* [1989] ECR 1839.

36. Case 27/86, *Constructions et Enterprises Industrielles S.A. (CEI) v. Association Intercommunale pour les Autoroutes des Ardennes*; case 28/86, *Ing.A. Bellini & Co. S.p.A. v. Regie de Bâtiments*; case 29/86, *Ing.A. Bellini & Co. S.p.A. v. Belgian State* [1987] ECR 3347.

37. See the *Transporoute* judgment in case 76/81, *loc. cit.* n. 33 above.

that his undertaking has the minimum funds, manpower and managerial staff required by the domestic law of the contracting authority, is compatible with Directive 71/305. Rejection of his tender by the awarding authority, if he fails to meet these domestic provisions, is legal even if the tenderer is recognized in a class equivalent to that required by domestic law governing the conditions of the contract to be awarded.

In 1987 a definition of 'authorities awarding contracts' was sought through an Article 177 reference by a Dutch court.[38] In particular, the court was requested to clarify whether a local land consolidation committee fell within the framework of article 1(b) of Directive 71/305. Pursuant to that provision, the state, regional or local authorities and legal persons governed by public law are to be regarded as 'authorities awarding contracts'. The consolidation committee in question had no legal personality, but its functions and composition were governed by legislation. The court interpreted the term 'state' in functional terms. It held that the aim of Directive 71/305, which is to ensure the effective attainment of freedom of establishment and freedom to provide services in respect of public works contracts, would be jeopardized if the provisions of the directive were to be held to be inapplicable, solely because a public works contract is awarded by a body, which although it is set up to carry out tasks entrusted to it by legislation, is not formally a part of the state's administration. Consequently, it considered the local consolidation committee, whose composition and function were laid down by legislation, and which depended on the authorities for the appointment of its members, the observance of its obligations arising out of its measures and the financing of the public works contracts which was its task to award, as falling within the notion of state for the purpose of the above-mentioned provision (article 1(b)), even though it is not part of the state administration in formal terms.[39] It is worth mentioning that under French and German administrative law the legal personality is a *conditio sine qua non* for a body exercising public administration on its own (which means that it is accountable before the competent forum). The court also ruled that a condition relating to the employment of long term unemployed persons is compatible with Directive

38. Case 31/87, *Gebroeders Beentjes B.V. v. State of Netherlands* [1988] ECR 4635.

39. See case 249/81, *Commission v. Ireland*, [1982] ECR 4005.

71/305, if it has no direct or indirect discriminatory effect on tenders from other member states,[40] and if it has been mentioned in the tender notice[41] – in other words, it must fall under article 29(4), which provides that an award may be based on criteria of a different nature within the framework of rules whose aim is to give preference to certain tenderers by way of aid (other than that in Article 90 EECT), on condition that the rules invoked are in conformity with the Treaty, in particular Article 92 *et seq*. Rejection of a contract on a contractor's inability to employ long-term unemployed persons has no relation to the checking of the contractor's suitability on the basis of his economic and financial standing and their technical knowledge and ability, or to the criteria for the award of contracts referred to in article 29 of Directive 79/305 (lowest-price tender or most economically advantageous offer). Derogation from this framework is permitted only with regard to preference schemes, which by definition have a discriminatory effect on tender competition for the award of a contract. It seems peculiar that the Court should have brought under the preference scheme exception (article 29(4)) clauses and conditions for the award of a contract, provided they have no direct or indirect discriminatory effect on contractors from other member states. (In other cases, the court did not permit clauses reserving a percentage of public procurement contracts to undertakings established in a particular area, on the grounds that they impede intra-Community trade, thus falling foul of Articles 30 and 90 EECT.) The court also said that the examination of a contractor's suitability based on its good standing and qualifications and its financial and economic standing may take place simultaneously with the award of a contract,[42] and reiterated that articles 20, 26 and 29 of Directive 71/305 are directly effective.

In 1988 an Italian court sought a preliminary ruling from the Court of Justice with respect to questions arising from a case pending before it.[43] In this case the court was requested to interpret article 29 of Directive 71/305 and pronounce on its direct effect. It held that rejection of a contract on the basis of mathematical criteria, without giving the tenderer an opportunity

40. In the USA it is a common practice to include such clauses in public procurement contracts. These are known as contract compliance clauses.
41. See *Bellini* case 28/86 [1987] ECR 3347.
42. *Ibid.*
43. Case 103/88, *Fratelli Costanzo S.p.A. v. Comune di Milano* [1989] ECR 1839.

to furnish information, is inconsistent with article 29(5) of the directive. The interpretation of the latter provision reveals its direct effectiveness[44] as it lays down a precise, detailed procedure for the examination of tenders which appear to be abnormally low. That aim would be jeopardized if member states were able, when implementing article 29(5), to depart from it to any material extent. The latter consideration may create interpretation problems with respect to the question of whether they appear to be abnormally low, and not only when they are obviously abnormally low. The court, following previous case law,[45] ruled that the contracting authorities must give an opportunity to tenderers to furnish explanations regarding the genuine nature of their tenders, when those tenders appear to be abnormally low and not only when they are obviously abnormally low. The court did not proceed to an analysis of the word 'obviously'. It rather seems that the term indicates the existence of precise and concrete evidence as to the abnormally low tender. The use of the word 'abnormally' implies a quantitative criterion, left at the discretion of the contracting authority. It should be borne in mind that efficient and highly competitive tenderers often submit 'abnormally' low tenders. It appears from both the wording and the aim of the directive that in both situations, contracting authorities should seek explanation and reject unrealistic offers, informing the Advisory Committee.[46] On the other hand, if the tender is just 'abnormally' low, it could be argued that it is within the discretion of the contracting authority to utilize article 29(5) to investigate the genuine offer of a tender. Perhaps relevant information and closer examination of the tender by the contracting authority on its own motion would suffice to award the contract without further explanations from the contractor.

In 1988, Italian courts sought a preliminary ruling from the ECJ in two cases. Both concerned supplies of pharmaceutical products to local health authorities. In the first one[47] the court determined

44. See also Case 31/87 *Gebroeders Beentjes B.V. v. State of Netherlands loc. cit.* n. 38 above.

45. Case 76/81 *Transporoute* [1982] ECR 417, *loc. cit.* n. 33 above.

46. The Advisory Committee for Public Procurement was set up by Decision 77/63 (OJ 1977, L13/15) and is composed of representatives of the member states belonging to the authorities of those states and has as its task to supervise the proper application of public procurement directives by member states.

47. Case 21/88, *Dupont de Nemours Italiana S.p.A v. Unita Sanitaria Locale No.2 di Carrara*, judgment of 20 March 1990.

the effect which a preferential system reserving to undertakings established in certain regions of a national territory a proportion of public supplies contracts is likely to have on the free movement of goods. The system of the reserved quota of public supply contracts falls foul of Article 30 EECT. It cannot be justified under the rule of reason of Article 36 EECT, nor under article 26 of Directive 77/62. It also stated that it is inconsistent with Article 30, even if it is considered as aid within the meaning of Article 92 EECT.

The second case[48] concerned whether the reservation of a proportion (30 per cent) of public supplies contracts to undertakings located in a specific area is incompatible with Article 30 EECT, even if the measures fall under Article 92 EECT.[49]

Another national case[50] concerning supplies of pharmaceutical products was the subject of an Article 177 reference by a Spanish court in 1989. In this case the interpretation of Articles 7, 30, 92(1) EECT, with regard to national rules providing for agreements between the social security authorities and representatives of the Spanish pharmaceutical industry for supplying those authorities, was requested by the European Court of Justice. The implementation of Directives 77/62 and 88/295 and their application in the case were also in issue. It was a very important case, as it was related to free movement of pharmaceutical products and drugs in the framework of social security schemes. The compatibility of the framework agreement with Community law and public procurement directives was not pronounced upon by the court, as the national litigation was withdrawn. The Commission, in its intervention in the case before the court, stated that it considered the framework agreement to be in breach of Community law (Article 30 EECT) and Directive 77/62. The Commission later brought an Article 169 EECT case against Spain on the subject.[51]

In 1989, the court gave a preliminary ruling to a question referred by the Tribunal Administratif of Versailles[52] concerning the right of a Portuguese company awarded a subcontract in France to move its workforce there in order to complete the

48. Case 351/88, *Lavatori Bruneau Slr. v. Unita Sanitaria Locale RM/24 di Monterotondo.*
49. The same judgment as in Case 21/88 *Dupont.*
50. Case 179/89, *Farmaindustria v. Consejeria de salud de la Junta de Andalucia*, pending.
51. See case 32/92, *Commission v. Spain loc. cit.* n. 27 above.
52. Case 113/89, *Rush Portugesa Lda v. Office National d'Imigration.*

project. The court ruled that under Articles 59 and 60 EECT and the Act of Accession of the Kingdom of Spain and the Portuguese Republic, France may not impose conditions relating to the recruitment of manpower *in situ* or obtaining of work permits for the Portuguese workforce.

Also in 1989, in a case[53] referred to it by an Italian court, the ECJ condemned the rejection of a works contract based on mathematical criteria, and also did not make any distinction between 'obviously abnormally low' and simply abnormally low offers.

In 1992 the Belgian Raad van Staat asked the European Court of Justice for a preliminary ruling on the interpretation of provisions within the Works Directives 71/305 and 71/304, which were in dispute in a case before the former.[54] The national litigation concerned a dispute on the past of a holding company against the Belgian State for failure to include the holding company in an official list of recognized contractors for future public works contracts, on the grounds that the holding company did not posses any technical expertise in relation to construction projects. The works directives require specific qualitative technical criteria for selection of tenderers (articles 23 to 26 of the Works Directive 71/305) and the official list of recognized contractors refers to these criteria (article 28 of the Works Directive 71/305). The court proceeded by endorsing the wide interpretation of the definition of works contracts under the original Works Directive 71/304 and under the amending Works Directive 88/295 and declared that even when an undertaking does not posses the relevant expertise to perform the actual works, contracting authorities by no means should exclude it from tendering procedures. The court also made reference to the explicit provision of group tendering through consortia and the obligation of contracting authorities to require specific legal personality for the group only after the award of the contract to that group.

Also in 1992, a Spanish court requested a preliminary ruling by the ECJ on the interpretation of the definition of works contracts under the relevant directive. The national case[55] was concerned

53. Case 296/89, *Impresa Dona Alfonso di Dona Alfonso & Figli s.n.c. v. Consorzio per lo Sviluppo Industriale del Comune di Monfalcone*, not reported.
54. Case C 389/92, *Ballast Nedam Groep NV v. Belgische Staat* [1994] 2 CMLR.
55. Case 331/92, *Gestion Hotelera Internacional S.A v. Comunidad Autonoma de Canarias* [1994] ECR 1.

with the installation and management of a casino and other leisure investment services in a hotel owned by a Spanish local authority. The relevant activities were advertised in the local press as two related contracts and the contracting authority had attached as a condition to the successful award of the contracts the carrying out of some unidentified construction work, which was ancillary to the performance of the main contracts. The construction involved was, in value, substantially lower than the value of the leisure, investment and management services required by the contract, and the court had no difficulty in declaring the inapplicability of the works directive. It referred to the definition of public works contracts, where, when the execution of works has incidental character with regard to the concession of goods or services the mixed contract in question was outside the scope of the works directive.

The impact of public procurement legislation after the completion of the Single Market

The regulation of public markets in the European Community has been recently rationalized with the adoption of 'consolidated' directives on works, supplies and utilities.[56] These legal instruments replace the previous directives, without altering the regime established by their predecessors. Qualification criteria with respect to contractors' eligibility and technical capacity and financial and economic standing should be homogeneously applied in public procurement sectors of the European Community. The post-internal market era has witnessed litigation which has been mainly concerned with the interpretation and clarification of provisions of European legislation on public procurement.

In 1993 a reference to the European Court of Justice was made by the High Court (Queens Bench Division) on, *inter alia,* the utilization of public procurement directives for the purchasing of pharmaceutical products (narcotic drugs previously being supplied under licence) by the competent health authorities.[57] The national court requested a preliminary ruling on the interpretation of article

56. Works Directive 93/37, OJ 1993, L199/1; Supplies Directive 93/36, OJ 1993, L199/54; Utilities Directive 93/38, OJ 1993 L199/84.
57. Case C 324/93, *R. v. The Secretary of State for the Home Department, ex p Evans Medical Ltd and Macfarlan Smith Ltd.*

25 of the Supplies Directive 77/62, particularly the meaning of 'most economically advantageous offer'. The national court asked whether factors concerning continuity and reliability as well as security of supplies fall under the framework of the 'most economically advantageous offer', when the latter is being evaluated. The Court of Justice, following previous case law,[58] reiterated the flexible and wide interpretation of the relevant award criterion and had no difficulty in declaring that contracting authorities may use the most economically advantageous offer as an award criterion by choosing the factors which they want to apply in evaluating tenders, provided these factors are mentioned, in hierarchical order, in the invitation to tender and/or the contract documents. Two member states intervened in the case and submitted that a restricted system of supply of potentially dangerous substances could be justified by having recourse to article 6(1) and (4) of the supplies directive, which permits the use of negotiated procedures when, for technical reasons, the supply of goods in question can be guaranteed by only a particular supplier (article 6(1)), or when, for security reasons, the supply of goods in question is declared secret, or when their delivery must be accompanied by the application of administrative laws or regulations that guarantee the secrecy of the delivery (article 6(4)).

In 1993 the Divisional Court of the Queens Bench Division of the Supreme Court made a reference to the European Court of Justice on the interpretation of Directive 90/531 concerning procurement in public utilities. The national case[59] concerned the definition of the relevant provision of the directive relating to the application of procurement rules to entities operating in the telecommunications sector. Article 8(1) of the utilities directive provides for an exemption from the regime and for the inapplicability of the directive, when contracting authorities in the telecommunications sector operate under substantially the same competitive conditions within the same geographical market. The national court asked for an interpretation of article 8(1) of the utilities directive and in particular the competence of member states to determine the sufficiently genuine competitive regime and the criteria for such evaluation, between telecommunications operators in a geographical area, in order to exclude them from

58. Case 31/87, *Gebroeders Beenjes v. The Netherlands* [1988] ECR 4635.
59. Case C 392/93, *The Queen and H.M. Treasury, ex p British Telecommunications PLC* OJ 1993, C 287/6 [1996] All ER (EC 411).

the application of the directive. Clarification was also requested as to the possibility of awards of damages to individuals in case of wrongful implementation of the relevant provision by member states. The court held that contracting entities themselves and not member states should determine the exemption of any telecommunications services by reference to matters of fact as well as of law (the characteristics of the services concerned, the existence of alternative services, the price factor, the market position of competitors and the existence of any legislative constraints). As the infringement was not a *manifest and serious breach* of community law[60], it was not required for the UK government to make reparation for any loss or damage.

In 1993 the Commission brought the Netherlands under an Article 169 EECT action before the European Court of Justice[61] for a failure to observe the supplies directive and particularly to specify, without discriminatory descriptions, the required goods for procurement. The Neerlands Inkoopcentrum NV had published a notice in the *Official Journal* for the procurement of a meteorological data processing system, which it specified with a particular trade mark, without using the term 'or equivalent'. The court, following its previous case law,[62] reiterated that article 7(6) of the Supplies Directive 77/62 (as amended by article 8 of Directive 89/295) intends to eliminate discriminatory description of supplies by utilization of particular trade marks, unless accompanied by the words 'or equivalent', and only then in cases where reference to the particular trade mark is necessary for the description of the product in question. The Court of Justice also pronounced the compulsory and unconditional character of point 7 of annex III to the Supplies Directive 77/62, which requires indication of authorized persons, date, time and place for the opening of tenders, in order to allow tenderers to identify their competitors and enable them to ensure that transparent and qualitative evaluation of their offers applies.

The same year the Commission brought Germany[63] before the European Court of Justice under Article 169 EECT for failure to implement correctly the public supplies and public works

60. See cases C 46/93, *Brasserie du Pecheur SA v Germany*, and C 48/93, *Regina v Secretary of State for Transport, ex p Factortame LTD*, [1996] 1 CMLR 889.
61. Case C 359/93, *Commission v. The Netherlands*, judgment of 24 January 1995.
62. Case 45/87, *Commission v. Ireland* [1988] ECR 4929.
63. Case C 443/93, *Commission v. Federal Republic of Germany*, judgment of 11 August 1995.

directives into its legal system. The case concerned with the appropriate legal instrument for such implementation, which must confer rights and duties to individuals. The German implementing provisions could be described as procedural orders to the competent authorities, which were not legally binding and which did not grant specific rights upon individuals. The court declared that such implementation infringed the Treaty and the relevant directives.

Nineteen ninety-four witnessed the initiation of interim measures by the Commission against Belgium[64] under Article 185 EECT in order to suspend the award of a contract relating to the purchase of buses for public transport in Wallonia. The Commission initiated Article 169 EECT proceedings against Belgium for infringement of the Utilities Directive 90/531, particularly the selection of tender offers and their evaluation. The substantive part of the case (Article 169 EECT) is still pending before of the Court of Justice, but the latter had the opportunity to reply to the Commissions request for interim measures. The Commission argued that interim measures with suspension of the award procedures were justified by conditions of manifest urgency dictated by the possibility of serious and irreparable damage and an aggrieved tenderer. The court, in balancing the interest of the parties in question, ruled that the performance and completion of the contract should take precedence over potential economic damage, on the grounds of public interest. The contract concerned the purchase and operation of new buses by a transport authority, and delays in its execution could seriously harm the lives of individuals – commuters who relied on the modernization of the transport fleet. The President of the Court refuse the interim measures requested.

In 1994 also the Commission brought two member states before the Court of Justice for infringement of procurement directives. The first case was against Italy[65] and concerned the award of motorway construction contracts outside the framework of the works directive. The court had not had the opportunity to pronounce on the failure of the Italian state to observe the provisions of the works directive in a similar case against Italy, which related to the same construction project, because that case was held inadmissible.[66] The Italian authorities justified the private award for the execution of the works contract in question on

64. Case C 87/94R, *Commission v. Belgium*, order of 22 April 1994.
65. Case C 57/94, *Commission v. Italy*, judgment of 18 May 1995.
66. Case 296/92, *Commission v. Italy*, judgment of 12 January 1994.

article 9(b) and (d) of the works directive, which provide for deviation from the award procedures stipulated in the directives, on the grounds of extreme urgency (article 9(d)) and technical reasons (article 9(b)). The court rejected both submissions based on a restrictive interpretation of article 9 of the works directive.

The second case was against Greece[67] for failure to comply with the supplies directive. The case concerned a framework agreement with suppliers to supply textiles to contracting authorities for a period, without any publication of the contracts in the *Official Journal*. The case in question presents similarities with previous litigation before the court, in which the latter condemned the operation of framework agreement as in breach of the supplies directive.[68] In the instant case, the court reiterated its condemnation and pronounced on the failure of the Greek state to observe the supplies directive.

Enforcement of public procurement directives

Public procurement directives have been introduced in order to establish the necessary conditions for the fulfilment of Treaty provisions relating to free movement of goods and services, to ensure equality of opportunities for those tendering for public contracts and, finally, to end discrimination based on nationality in the award of contracts.

The public procurement sector is by nature decentralized and requires a decentralized control. In some member states there are already remedies for breach of public procurement laws, and it is the responsibility of all the member states to provide legal remedies to the parties concerned capable of enforcing the provisions of the public procurement directives.

The aim of the European institutions should be to provide for the possibility of having uniform remedies in all member states, of harmonizing procedures or at least of coordinating national laws and administrative provisions relating to the application of procedures for reviewing public procurement contracts. Uniformity of application, as far as legal remedies are concerned, is a desirable situation but it is an ideal which is difficult to achieve, since there are different ways, already established, for solving public procurement disputes. It is almost impossible to

67. Case 79/94, *Commission v. Greece* judgment of 4 May 1995.
68. Case C 32/92, *Commission v. Spain* [1994] I ECR 1569.

have one law applicable in all member states, due to separate legal traditions and procedures. Any attempt to abolish existing national systems would be extremely difficult, not to say a waste of time.

Similarly, harmonization of national procedures concerning the availability of legal remedies for breach of public procurement contracts is neither possible nor necessary. In order to achieve harmonization, that is approximation of national legal orders, one should start from a common point; in other words, the national legal orders to be harmonized should be homogeneous.

In the case of public procurement, the existing national remedies are addressed to national or administrative courts or administrative bodies or arbitrators. Furthermore, the national law applicable in each member state varies from pure civil to pure public administrative law. Finally, the cost of initiating proceedings differs from member state to member state, depending on the cost of living or the judicial cost in each country. Under those conditions, it is hardly possible to achieve harmonization. What remains is to coordinate these national legal remedies with a view to ensuring a procedure and a sanction for the application of the underlying public procurement directives.

The measures to be taken by member states

In line with the compliance directive and the enforcement regime of public procurement legislation, member states should be left to implement procedures consistent with their own judicial practices to achieve effective and rapid review rules. This approach is consistent with the provisions in Article 189 EECT, that a directive shall be binding as to the result to be achieved, leaving the form and the methods to the discretion of the member states. In some member states, highly developed systems of monitoring public procurement procedures already exist. Both directives aim at coordinating existing procedures and procedures to be introduced with a view to a uniform application of the underlying directives concerning public supplies, public works, and utilities. It seems that neither directive has direct effect.

However, by virtue of article 2 of Directive 89/665 and article 2 of Directive 92/13, the measures concerning the review procedures shall include interim measures, by way of interlocutory procedures, with the aim of correcting the alleged infringement or preventing further damages. Provision shall be made for measures to suspend or to ensure the suspension of the procedure for the award of a public contract or the implementation of any decision taken by the contracting authority. In most of the member states, suspension would be effected by an injunction. National courts have the power to grant injunction to restrain unlawful acts.

It should be borne in mind that a suspension of the whole procedure or of the implementation of any decision will create some problems. First, review procedures should not have an automatic suspensive character. Indeed, Article 2(3) in both directives reads so. Secondly, in practical terms, a disappointed tenderer could ask the court to order the procuring authority to reconsider its bid and not to enter into a contract in the meantime. In many cases, this would cause disproportionate hardship. Therefore, the national courts or administrative bodies should take into account the probable consequences to all interests likely to be harmed, as well as the public interest. In fact, article 2(4) in both instruments introduces a proportionality principle, meaning that where any grant of a review measure causes negative consequences, such consequences shall not exceed the benefits. For the sake of history, it is worth mentioning that article 3 of the draft Directive 89/665 (COM(88) 733 fin.) gave the Commission the right to suspend a contract award procedure for a period of up to three months. Since this would have led to legal uncertainty, as at the same time national courts have suspensive powers, it has been deleted from the final text.

In addition to interim measures correcting the alleged infringement or suspending the award procedure, article 2(1)(b) provides for measures to set aside unlawfully taken decisions by the contracting authority, including the removal of discriminatory technical, economic or financial specifications in the invitation to tender, the contract document or any other document relating to the award procedure. The present texts of the directives are not sufficiently clear in respect to the execution of the contract itself. It could be argued that contracts might be set aside, even after having been awarded. The effect of annulling contracts would be to render uncertain for several years the basis for proceeding with important public works and could cause damage extending well beyond the authority under challenge. The Commission has made clear its intention that contracts once awarded should not be put at risk of being overturned. However, the fact of setting aside a decision leaving the contract unaffected causes serious doubts as to the validity of the contract. In some continental legal orders, the theory of detachable acts has been developed and permits the validity of administrative acts leading to the making of a contract to be considered distinct from the contract itself and for them to be open to challenge on grounds of their illegality, without affecting the validity of the contract. In these legal orders, the attack of the unlawful decision is a prerequisite to moving for damages. In other jurisdictions, the setting aside of the decision without touching the contract will create problems, as the legal basis of the contract has been removed.

It is the discretion of the national court to decide whether it should set aside the decision to enter into a contract or simply to declare illegalities in the award procedure and therefore grant damages. Directive 92/13 recognizes explicitly the theory of detachable acts and provides in article 2(d) that, prior to an award of damages, the contested decision must first be set aside or declared illegal.

The power to order the removal of discriminatory specifications in the contract documents is a different matter. Such an order should not be made in a way which would hinder the procurement process and it should ensure that the procedure is in accordance with the principle of non-discrimination.

The award of damages

Article 2(1)(c) in both directives provides for the award of damages to persons harmed by an infringement of public procurement law. The purpose behind this provision is to mobilize the interested contractors in order to supervise the application of public procurement directives. In addition, damages as financial consequences control in a very immediate way contract officers, their superiors and their financial control authorities.

As already mentioned, European law does not require the provision of a remedy for damages in case of a breach of a directly effective Union rule. The reasons for that absence vary: in some cases the national court has held that the authority in breach of Union law did not owe any obligation directly to the plaintiff or that the plaintiff's losses were the results of foreseeable economic risk; in others, the award of damages has been seen as an unacceptable fetter on the freedom of authorities to enact legislative measures or administrative rules in good faith, pursuant to their general duty to safeguard public interest, such as human health. Damages may be available as a consequence of provi sions of national law which make a national authority liable to compensate for breach of its obligations. Procuring authorities are subject to a duty to observe European rules and are liable for damages in breach of those rules. In the context of the compliance directives, a question arises as to whether an aspirant contractor seeking damages should prove that it would have been accepted as a tenderer or would have won the contract, if not for the infringement.

Under the restrictive procedures, a limited number of contractors or suppliers are invited to tender pursuant to article 22 of the public works directive, or article 19 of the public supplies directive. Where a contractor or a supplier has applied as a candidate, but has not been invited to tender and the contracting authority has infringed the directive, the assessment of loss would be difficult since tender costs have not been incurred and the contractor or supplier might not, in any event, have been awarded the contract.

In the case that a tender has been submitted, it may be easier to show that a quantifiable loss has been suffered by the contractor or supplier in respect of which it should be indemnified, at least so far as the expenses of tendering are concerned. Any additional loss would be more difficult to prove. Under the utilities compliance directive, the undertaking claiming damages must prove the infringement of public procurement law and the effect of this infringement on its chance of being awarded the contract. It does not have to prove that, in the absence of the infringement it would have been awarded the contract.

Where the complaint is that the procuring authority has failed to accept the most economically advantageous tender, as required by the procurement directives, there is probably no alternative; the procuring authority will be required to advise unsuccessful tenders of the reason for their failure. Then, it is for the unsuccessful tenders to assess whether these reasons are so defective as to justify legal proceedings for compensation. It should be recalled that the criteria laid down in the procurement directives are wide-ranging, leaving a great deal of discretion to the contracting authority. The burden of proof will be on the unsuccessful tenderer to persuade the court that its tender was more economically advantageous than that of the winning tender. On the other hand, where the potential tenderer complains of unlawful exclusion from the tendering process, it should be entitled, on proof, to recovery of costs actually incurred, which will usually not be substantial. Under the draft compliance directive on utilities sectors, the amount of damages refunded should be deemed to be 1 per cent of the value of the contract, where a contractor is preparing a bid or participating in an award procedure, unless it proves that its costs were greater. This provision has been deleted from the final text of Directive 92/13. It should be noted that the draft Directive 89/665 mentioned three grounds of action for damages: the cost of unnecessary studies, forgone profits and lost opportunities. The final text of the directive, interestingly, remains silent and refers only to award of damages generally (article 2(1)(c)). There have been fears that the inclusion of forgone profits and lost opportunities could have led to speculative and wasteful litigation.

There are two observations relating to damages litigation in public procurement. First, as it is generally admitted, undertakings will be hesitant to bring a contracting authority before a court, since they will want to maintain good relations in the future. Litigation between a supplier and a contracting authority tantamounts to an irrevocable break of their relation. Secondly, if damages are too greatly and too readily awarded, public contracting authorities will find themselves proceeding so extremely carefully as to seriously impede any public work or supplies contract.

It remains to be seen how, in practice, national courts will deal with the matter. Since there are sixteen different jurisdictions throughout the Union – those of the fifteen member states, plus the jurisdiction of the European Community as the 'new legal order' – most probably there will be great differences in the amounts awarded as compensation by national courts. This could prevent some undertakings from taking any proceedings in member states that provide for low sanctions. In this case, the member state is obliged to introduce more effective procedures, similar though not necessarily identical to those of the rest of the Union. The Commission should launch an action under Article 169 EECT to have the ECJ declare that a member state has not conformed with the compliance directive.

The directives provide that member states should establish judicial or administrative bodies responsible for their enforcement. Member states, therefore, have a choice as to the forum and procedures provided for hearing disputes or otherwise achieving the required result. In addition, they require that all decisions taken by bodies responsible for review procedures shall be effectively enforced.

Since contracting authorities are involved in a public contract, in many continental jurisdictions public law will be applied and the dispute is to be addressed before administrative courts. In other cases, civil law applies in public procurement litigation, while in the Netherlands, there is a remarkably swift arbitration system for building contracts. Consequently, the question of enforcement of the decisions is relevant to the choice of the forum. Normally, national courts have the power, the prerogative and the means to enforce their decisions. An administrative body, without judicial powers to order discovery or injunctions, could not ensure effective enforcement of its decisions. In case of arbitration, the winning party, in order to have the arbitration award enforced, has to go before national courts and exhaust the relevant proceedings. Moreover, there are some doubts as to the consistency of tribunals' decisions. National courts are skilled at construing contracts and statutory provisions, knowledgeable about the principles of damages and staffed by judges. On the other hand, an administrative body or a tribunal, normally staffed by lawyers and laymen experienced in public procurement, is a swift, flexible and rapid institution with simple proceedings to resolve disputes, since it will deal exclusively with this matter.

The European Commission's role

As mentioned above, under the draft Directive 89/665, the Commission had extensive powers, namely to intervene in an administrative or judicial procedure and to suspend unilaterally the procedure for award of a public procurement contract. Those powers were indeed far beyond the provision of Article 100A EEC Treaty and could only be justified under Article 235 EECT. The Commission's intervention was a novel provision, since it has no power to be a party or to intervene in a trial before national courts. The *vires* of this provision was questioned, since the draft directive was unclear at that particular point; it did not specify whether the Commission would have had a certain right to intervene or whether its intervention was subject to invitation or the permission of the court. In the latter case, it would have been considered as an *amicus curiae*, advising the court upon the proper interpretation of Union law. On the other hand, it could be argued that the Commission's intervention would have been desirable, since it can only be heard in case of interim measures before the Court of Justice or under the proceedings of Article 169 EECT. Interim measures may be taken by the court only if the case in question is pending before it, and an Article 169 action is a heavy, cumbersome and time-consuming procedure, as far as public procurement cases are concerned.

The Commission's suspension power could lead to legal uncertainty and undermine the independence of the courts. Control by both court and the Commission simultaneously is not desirable. In the final text of Directive 89/665, all these powers have been deleted and the Commission has been left with the right to invoke the article 3 procedure by way of notification of an infringement of Union provisions to a member state requiring its correction. The same regime is provided for in Directive 92/13 (article 8). Interestingly, the Commission's action is limited. It can only notify a clear and manifest infringement of Union provisions, in the field of public procurement, before a contract has been concluded. The former requirement introduces a kind of qualitative test. Clear and manifest infringement probably means an outspoken breach of a relevant provision. Unclear and ambiguous situations will fall outside the scope of the notification procedure. The latter requirement serves the principle of legal certainty, since after the contract has been concluded, it is extremely costly and undesirable to start investigating it, probably with a view to suspending it.

After 21 days in the case of Directive 89/665, and 30 days in the case of Directive 92/13, from the Commission's notification to a member state, the latter is obliged to communicate to the former: (i) its confirmation that an infringement has been corrected, or (ii) a justification as to why no correction has been made, or (iii) a notice that a suspension of the award procedure has been ordered. When the suspension is lifted, the member state is obliged to inform the Commission. It is apparent that the Commission's role has been limited on the insistence of member states and from a power to intervene or to suspend award procedures, it has been left with the mere possibility of notification.

There have been two cases[69] so far in which the Commission utilized the procedure provided in article 3 of Directive 89/665. The ECJ had the opportunity to declare that the special procedure

69. Case C 359/93, *Commission v. The Netherlands*, judgment of 24 January 1995; case 79/94, *Commission v. Greece*, judgment of 4 May 1995.

of article 3 is a preliminary measure which can neither derogate from nor replace the powers of the Commission to initiate proceedings under Article 169 EECT. In both cases, the communication of the Commissions position under article 3 of Directive 89/665 served as the reasoned opinion for the subsequent compliance proceedings under Article 169 EECT.

Where the Commission's role is really novel is under Directive 92/13, where provision has been made for a conciliation procedure, apart from the attempt to achieve an amicable settlement laid down in article 1(3), as an endeavour to avoid any litigation between the parties. The conciliation procedure shall be distinguished from the judicial/administrative procedures at national level. Interestingly, there is no provision concerning the relationship between the two proceedings, and in the event that the same person were to initiate conciliation and judicial review proceedings under the directive simultaneously, the relation between them is unclear. Article 11(2)(a) of the directive stipulates that conciliation proceedings shall be without prejudice to proceedings under Articles 169 or 170 EECT and the rights of the parties or any other person under national laws (article 11(2)(b)). Any person having an interest and feeling that a breach of relevant public procurement law rules has occurred, may notify the Commission or the competent authorities of a member state. The possibility of the interested person choosing either the Commission or a Member State's authorities creates some uncertainty, since it is admitted that the whole public procurement problem is decentralized. The Commission or the national authorities may refer the case to the Advisory Committee for Public Contracts[70] or the Advisory Committee on Telecommunications.[71] These Committees will set up working groups with a view to reaching an agreement between the parties.

70. This Committee has been set up by EC Council Decision 71/306 (OJ 1971, L185) as amended by EC Council Decision 77/63 (OJ 1977, L152).
71. See art 31 of EEC Dir 90/531.

CHAPTER FIVE

The interplay between the regulation of public procurement and European Union policies

As with every form of public spending, public procurement has an impact on other government policies. The application of public purchasing as an instrument in implementing related policies has been a bone of contention in member states, as is evident in the case law of the European Court of Justice, which has condemned national laws and administrative practices that allowed the use of public procurement as a tool of policy.

Three main government policies are closely related with public procurement and are the subject of the following analysis: regional development policy, social policy and, finally, industrial policy. These policies have been promoted through preferential or strategic public purchasing in the past, although the enactment of the public procurement legislation now leaves little margin for perpetuation of such approaches. However, provisions in the European directives and rulings of the European Court of Justice invite further examination of the interaction of public procurement with related policies.

Public procurement and regional development policy

A possible way of combating recession and its side effects (industrial decline, unemployment, social exclusion) is the enhancement of regionalism and the development of decentralized policies that can boost peripheral growth in the economy. A scenario such as this will need to incorporate not only the commitment of a central government towards regional economic development, but also the participation of local and regional authorities in implementing the strategic plan. Regionalism and spatial economic development should focus on incentives aiming at growth and optimal allocation of resources, always within a regime of workable and effective competition. Regional development policies, centralized or decentralized, should have as a priority agenda small- and medium-sized enterprises, which are often located in less favoured regions, or regions of economic decline and industrial restructuring. The idea behind the above policies is to promote and enhance the market performance and participation of small and medium firms in order to achieve economic growth within a region. The concentration of policy-makers on small- and medium-sized firms could also be justified by the fact that in real terms they represent the vast majority of businesses within the European economies.

Large firms often lack flexibility in adapting their strategies to new market requirements, where industrial restructuring in most cases has taken the form of voluntary or compulsory redundancies and workforce cuts. On the other hand, small firms appear more flexible in changes as they diversify their activities more effectively than large firms, without the need to have necessary recourse to labour cuts. It has been suggested that economic recovery from the present recession will emerge from the small enterprises which will first detect the signals of growth.

The policies which aim to assist small- and medium-sized enterprises focus on participation incentives in the markets,[1] the latter being defined as private or public markets. These policies adopt regionalism as their objective and endeavour to promote a decentralized economic growth through the periphery.[2] Regional policies are sophisticated measures aiming at optimal allocation of resources throughout a state and equal distribution of income among its citizens. Small- and medium-sized enterprises occupy a large share in European economies[3] and should be considered as one of the most important factors of Europe's industrial policy.

In this chapter, after establishing the link between SMEs, public purchasing and regional development policies, we will examine the performance of small and medium enterprises in public

1. European Commission, *Action Programme for SMEs* (COM(86) 445).
2. European Commission, *Public Procurement: Regional and Social Aspects* (COM(89) 400).
3. Commission of the European Communities, *SME TASK FORCE: SMEs and Public Procurement*, Brussels, 1988.

procurement, and attempt to determine the variables that affect their participation in the award of public contracts, as well as to provide suggestions and recommendations on the perception of public procurement as a tool of promoting regional development policies at domestic and European levels.

The importance of SMEs for European member states

The completion of the internal market should take into account the needs of economic and social cohesion. The latter have been defined as 'New Policy Areas' in the Commission's White Paper and the Single European Act. The policies which are associated with economic and social cohesion cover regional development in the European Union and define the economic function of federalism in practice. Not only are transfers from the centre to the periphery covered, but also the creation of a decentralized decision-making in adopting and implementing instruments that aim to reduce regional disparities and to promote employment in the least advantaged regions and in areas of industrial decline.

The economic importance of small- and medium-sized enterprises (SMEs) in the market[4] could be attributed to their ability to:

- increase efficiency and enhance macroeconomic growth;
- promote industrial restructuring and adjustment;
- create the opportunity for industrial and sectoral exploitation of particular skills and advantages;
- facilitate better allocation of resources and more equal income distribution.

In the European Union as a whole, SMEs account for a remarkable 95 per cent of the total number of enterprises. Their commercial activities represent 64 per cent of the annual turnover in the Union and they employ 70 per cent of the total workforce in Europe. In the United Kingdom, small and medium enterprises represent 99 per cent of the total number of enterprises and they account for 50 per cent of the country's annual turnover. They employ 65 per cent of the workforce.[5]

4. European Commission, *Promoting SME Participation in the Community* (COM(90) 166).
5. Commission of the European Communities, *Pan European Forum on Sub-Contracting in the Community*, Brussels, 1993.

The participation of SMEs in public sector contracts accounts for 2.2 per cent of the European Union's GDP and amounts to approximately ECU 94 bn. This is translated to 15.3 per cent of the share of the total participation of enterprises in public procurement. Bearing in mind the economic magnitude of public procurement in Europe (15 per cent of the European Union's GDP and approximately ECU 560 bn), it appears that although SMEs represent the vast majority of firms in Europe and are responsible for almost two-thirds of the annual turnover, their share in public markets is limited.

Although the opening up of protected public procurement markets and the liberalization of the public sector of the European member states have been defined as priority objectives not only for the completion of the Common Market but also for the proper functioning of global markets, they pose serious obstacles and to some extent threats for small- and medium-sized firms.[6] SMEs have often relied on regional preferences or other types of protectionism; they have developed long-standing dependency relations with very limited numbers of buyers, and their low competitiveness and quality, augmented by the lack of economies of scale and the inefficient mobility of labour, capital and know-how, constitute a real threat. SMEs need extensive preparation in order to enter public markets. They need to adapt to high technical standards rather than depend on traditional relationships with established purchasers, which then will open their horizons to larger geographical markets. They have to familiarize themselves with the procedural requirements stipulated by European and United Kingdom legislation and ensure that they meet quality assurance standards. Finally, they have to adopt and develop sophisticated marketing and management structures specifically designed for public sector contracts, a strategy which will be of substantial assistance to their future competitiveness.[7]

Policy-makers at both domestic and European levels face a dilemma in their attempts to promote the participation of SMEs in public procurement.[8] The dilemma lies in the choice of the most

6. European Commission, *SMEs participation in public procurement in the European Community* (SEC(92) 722).

7. G. O'Brien, 'Public Procurement and the Small or Medium Sized Enterprise', *Public Procurement Law Review*, 1993, Vol. 2, p.82.

8. *The Internal Market after 1992 - Meeting the Challenge*. Report to the E.C. Commission by the High Level Group on the Internal Market (Sutherland), November 1992.

appropriate framework for the promotion of SMEs' participation in tendering procedures and the award of public contracts.

The principal factors which have been claimed to inhibit SMEs in public procurement[9] include the relatively large size of the contracts, the difficulty in obtaining adequate information on forthcoming contracts, the shortage of language skills particularly in technical areas, the availability of time and the costs involved in preparing bids, the scarce management resources, problems relating to specification of standards,[10] difficulties in certification in other member states and obtaining quality assurance in other member states, difficulties in achieving credibility in another member state and, finally, delays in payment.[11]

The most effective way to stimulate SMEs' participation in public procurement and to ensure for them a fair share of the awarded public contracts has been achieved through the operation of preference schemes.[12] In the United Kingdom, preference schemes have taken the form of administrative practices, which although non-obligatory, were general in practice. There have been general preference schemes under which, when price and other considerations in offers were equal, the contract was awarded to enterprises established in listed development areas. Special preference schemes guaranteed a percentage of public contracts to enterprises established in Northern Ireland, or gave a price percentage advantage to enterprises that benefited employment in Northern Ireland.[13] So far, these schemes have been indissolubly linked with regional development policies, but since the completion of the Single Market in 1992 they have been abolished, as they are deemed to contravene directly or indirectly the basic principle of non-discrimination on grounds of nationality stipulated in the Treaty of Rome. Impact assessment studies

9. European Commission, *SMEs participation in public procurement in the European Community* (SEC(92) 722); European Commission *Action Programme for SMEs* (COM(86) 445); European Commission, *Public Procurement: Regional and Social Aspects* (COM(89) 400); European Commission, *Promoting SME Participation in the Community* (COM(90) 166).

10. European Commission Recommendation (91/561/EEC) of 24 October, 1991, on the standardization of notices of public contracts [1991] OJ 217.

11. Commission Staff Working Paper on the problem of the time taken to make payments in commercial transactions (SEC(92) (214)).

12. European Commission, *Public Procurement: Regional and Social Aspects* (COM(89) 400).

13. S. Arrowsmith, 'Public Procurement as an Instrument Policy and the Impact of Market Liberalisation', *The Law Quarterly Review*, 1995, Vol.11, p. 235.

undertaken by the European Commission[14] showed that the operation of preference schemes had a minimal effect on the economies of the regions where they had been applied, both in terms of the volume of procurement contracts, as well as in terms of real economic growth attributed to the operation of such schemes.

There is a great deal of controversy at European level as to whether preference schemes could ever conform with European law and policy. There are suggestions that the operation of such schemes violates fundamental principles of the Treaty of Rome, such as the free movement of goods, the right of establishment and the freedom to provide services; there is also the blunt violation of the principle of discrimination on grounds of nationality. On the other hand, the Treaty itself stipulates provisions for economic and social cohesion and regional policy. There is also the provision of state aids, within the limitations imposed by competition law and policy. Where, under this frame, do preference schemes fit? One could suggest that the utilization of preference schemes may fall under the ambit of state aids, which under the Treaty of Rome and the Maastricht Treaty are perfectly legitimate, provided they do not contravene the principles, law and policy of competition in the Common Market. There is room even to suggest that, if preference schemes, according to European Commission data, appear to have had a minimal effect on the market performance of firms in the public sector, their actual or potential effect on competition should be minimal. Thus a *de minimis* formula could be applied. Its is important here to reiterate that the application of preference schemes, if properly planned, can achieve a desirable spatial policy at both domestic and European levels.[15]

The European Commission had declared the temporary character of such schemes and explicitly abolished them after the completion of the Single Market. Preference schemes should be replaced by incentives for the participation of SMEs in public markets. These incentives should be backed up with clear and understandable policies and, of course, legislation. Indeed, the European Union has realized the importance of the above

14. European Commission, *Public Procurement: Regional and Social Aspects* (COM(89) 400).

15. For a thorough analysis, see J.M. Fernadez Martin and O. Stehmann, 'Product Market Integration versus Regional Cohesion in the Community', *European Law Review*, 1991, Vol. 16, p. 216.

transition from preference schemes to incentives for regional firms' participation in public procurement. Apart from a number of Communications to the Council of Ministers referring to the issue of SMEs in the European integration context, it has, in its legislation on public procurement, introduced provisions that could be regarded as a hybrid form of legislation on the SME in public procurement. All directives on public procurement, influenced by the European Commission's Communications, encourage the use of subcontracting in the award of public contracts. Particularly in public supplies contracts, the contracting entity in the invitation to tender may ask the tenderers on their intention to subcontract part of the contract to third parties. This reveals the importance of subcontracting for regional development in public procurement.[16] In public works contracts, contracting authorities awarding the principal contract to a concessionaire may require the concessionaire to subcontract to third parties at least 30 per cent of the total work provided for by the principal contract. Additionally, the subdivision by public entities of contracts into lots could facilitate SME participation. Finally, the reduction of the cost of tendering for public contracts through the introduction of simplified and standardized procedures will give SMEs an equal access to public contracts.

A number of suggestions[17] that might take the form of legislation or policy by either national or European authorities with a view to overcoming the above obstacles and promoting regional economic development through the strategic application of public procurement have been proposed. It should be mentioned that these suggestions find their origin in the spirit and to some extent the wording of the directives, but the relevant provisions cannot form the appropriate framework for their successful implementation. All the recommendations proposed have their advantages and disadvantages and the attempt to select one or more brings into play questions of legal compatibility, particularly with reference to European Community law.

(i) *Creation of certain thresholds in the European public*

16. D. Mardas, 'Sub-contracting, Small and Medium Sized Enterprises (SMEs) and Public Procurement in the European Community', *Public Procurement Law Review*, 1994, Vol. 3, CS 19.
17. C. Bovis, *Public Procurement and Small and Medium Sized Enterprises in the United Kingdom and the Republic of Ireland,* ACCA, Research Paper 17, 1996.

procurement directives for SMEs only. This will guarantee a certain percentage of public contracts to SMEs, but at the same time will exclude them from large public contracts. However, such a scheme would also pose considerable administrative difficulties in its implementation.

(ii) *Provisions that impose on contracting entities minimum target number of contracts for SMEs by means of a positive obligation for awarding authorities to divide a certain percentage of public contracts into lots and to require successful tenderers to subcontract a certain part of the contract.* Such provisions could improve SMEs' chances of participation in and award of public contracts, although they may contravene public procurement directives by avoiding the stipulated contract value thresholds.

(iii) *Preference in favour of SMEs in certain areas by means of price advantage or government subsidies.* The advantage could be the limitation of regional disparities and provision of a minimum of financial security in certain industries in certain regions, but is should be recalled that preference schemes have been abolished since 1993 as incompatible with the Single Market. Subsidies may be incompatible with Article 92 EU Treaty

Public procurement and social policy

In line with the above considerations discussing possible links between public procurement and the implementation of regional development policies, one should not overlook the implications of public purchasing on social policy in member states and the European Union as a whole. The social policy dimension of public procurement focuses primarily on employment concerns, whereby placing public contracts in a strategic way, goals such as social cohesion, combating of long-term unemployment and achievement of acceptable standards of living could be fostered.[18] However, it should be stated at the outset that the underlying objectives of the European regime on public procurement relating to enhanced competition and unobstructed market access in the public sector appear incompatible with the social dimension of European

18. See J. Carr, *New Roads to Equality: Contract Complianace for the United Kingdom,* Fabian Society, No. 517. Also, Institute of Personnel Management, *Contract Compliance: The United Kingdom Experience,* 1987.

integration, particularly in an era where recession and economic stagnation have revealed unemployment as the main characteristic of that integration.

The social policy considerations in relation to public procurement have been associated with the term 'contract compliance'. The concept is well known in North American jurisdictions,[19] as it has been in operation for some time in an attempt to reduce race and minorities inequalities in the market. For European jurisdictions, contract compliance could best be defined as the range of second-line policies relating to public procurement, which aim to combat discrimination on grounds of sex, race, religion or disability.[20] Contract compliance legislation and policy is familiar to most European member states, although the enactment of public procurement directives has changed the situation dramatically.[21] The completion of the Single Market and the priorities in achieving an acceptable degree of liberalization of the basic freedoms described in the Treaty of Rome have influenced national administration to a large extent in rethinking the whole issue of contract compliance and questions on its compatibility *vis-à-vis* fundamental principles of European law.[22]

The position of European institutions on contract compliance has been expressed in two cases before the European Court of Justice,[23] where its possible utilisation in public procurement by contracting authorities was examined. Contract compliance with reference to employment cannot be used as a selection criterion in tendering procedures. The selection of tenderers is based on a list of technical and financial requirements contained in the relevant directives and is exhaustive. This decision of the court touched the subject of positive approach within contract compliance – in other

19. For a detailed analysis see P.E. Morris, 'Legal Regulation of Contract Compliance: an Anglo-American Comparison', *Anglo-American Law Review*, 1990, Vol.19.

20. See ILEA Contract Compliance Equal Opportunities Unit, *Contract Compliance: a brief history,* 1990, London.

21. For example, in the United Kingdom, every initiative relating to contract compliance has been outlawed by virtue of the 1988 Local Government Act. Contract compliance from a public law perspective has been examined by T.Daintith, in 'Regulation by Contract: the new prerogative', CLP, 1979, Vol. 32.

22. See S. Arrowsmith, 'The Legality of Secondary Procurement Policies under the Treaty of Rome and the Works Directive', *Public Procurement Law Review*, 1992, Vol. 1. p. 410.

23. See case C 360/89, *Commission v. Italy,* judgment of 3 July 1992; case 31/87, *Gebroeders Beentjes B.V v. The Netherlands* [1989] ECR 4365.

words, measures and policies imposed by contracting authorities on tenderers as suitability criteria for their selection in public procurement contracts. Such positive action measures and policies intend to complement the actual objectives of public procurement which are confined in economic and financial parameters and are based on a transparent and predictable legal background. The court (and the European Commission) were reluctant in accepting such an over-flexible interpretation of the procurement directives and based on the literal interpretation of the relevant provisions, disallowed positive actions of a social policy dimension as part of the selection criteria for tendering procedures in public procurement. However, it should be mentioned that contract compliance can incorporate not only unemployment considerations, but also promote equality of opportunities and eliminate sex or race discrimination in the relevant market. Indeed, the directives on public procurement stipulate that the contracting authority may require tenderers to observe national provisions of employment legislation when they submit their offers. The ability to observe and conform with national employment laws in a member state may constitute a ground of disqualification and exclusion of the defaulting firm from public procurement contracts. In fact, under such interpretation, contract compliance may be a factor of selection criteria specified in the directives, as it contains a negative approach (obey, otherwise be excluded) to legislation and measures relating to social policy.[24]

On the other hand, in another case,[25] the ECJ ruled that social policy considerations, can only be part of award criteria in public procurement, and especially in cases where the most economically advantageous offer is selected. The court accepted that the latter award criterion contains factors and parameters that are not exhaustively defined in the directives. It should be mentioned that contract compliance can be utilized only when it is part of a contractual obligation of the public contract and does not run contrary to the basic principles of the Treaty.

Contract compliance in public procurement needs to be addressed at policy- and law-making levels, particularly in the light

24. It should be mentioned that adherence to health and safety laws has been considered by a British court as part of the technical requirements specified in the works directive for the process of selection of tenderers; see *General Building and Maintenance v. Greenwich Borough Council* [1993] IRLR 535.

25. Case 31/87, *Gebroeders Beenjes B.V v. The Netherlands* [1989] ECR 4365.

of the Inter-governmental Conference of 1996. With so much at stake, in regulating the public procurement markets of the member states, the social policy dimensions of such exercise should be carefully discoursed at Community level and the impact of its implementation through public purchasing should be thoroughly weighted. There are arguments both in favour of and against incorporating social policy considerations in public procurement. The most important argument in favour focuses on the ability of public procurement to promote parts of the member states' social policy, with particular reference to long-term unemployment, equal distribution of income, social exclusion and protection of minorities. Under such a positively oriented approach, public purchasing could be regarded as an instrument of policy in the hands of national administrations with a view to rectifying social equilibria.

Contract compliance in public procurement could also cancel the stipulated aims and objectives of the liberalization of the public sector in the European Union. The regulation of public markets focuses on economic considerations and competition. Adherence to social policy factors could derail the whole process, as the public sector will pay more for its procurement by extra or hidden cost in the implementation of contract compliance in purchasing policies.

Public procurement and industrial policy

The implementation of industrial policies through public purchasing focuses on either the sustainment of strategic national industries, or the development of infant industries. In both cases, preferential purchasing patterns can provide the economic and financial framework for the development of such industries, at the expense of competition and free trade. Although the utilization of public procurement as a means of industrial policy in member states may breach directly or indirectly primary Treaty provisions on free movement of goods and the right of establishment and the freedom to provide services, it is far from clear whether the European Commission and the ECJ could accept public procurement as a means of state aid. In the light of the *Du Pont de Nemours* case,[26] a possibility appears of qualifying the pursuit of

26. Case C 21/88, *Du Pont de Nemours Italiana SpA v. Unita Sanitaria Locale N.2 di Carrara*, [1990] ECR 889.

industrial policies in member states through public procurement as state aid.[27]

Industrial policies are closely associated with the development of methods and strategies which can promote industrial restructuring and adjustment in less favoured regions. Apart from grants and other forms of financial assistance, which rather constitute a passive form of restructuring process, as less favoured regions throughout the Union are in receipt of financial assistance without any direct or indirect involvement, or with very limited involvement in industrial restructuring, public procurement represents a viable option within the constraints imposed by the Single Market and the competitive regime that is affiliated with it. Participation in public markets indicates a direct form of industrial restructuring and adjustment, as less favoured regions can benefit significantly form such a process.

Grants and direct financial assistance from member states or from European Union funds perpetuate the suboptimal division of the European Union into different types of region. It could be maintained that instead of encouraging economic growth and economic alignment of less favoured regions with developed ones, they continue to support uncompetitively peripheral areas in Europe. Public procurement as a form of state aid in pursuit of industrial policy objectives can benefit industies which are located in less favoured regions. Such industries may not have access to opportunities for specialization and to know-how, which constitute an enormous advantage and reinforce the position of the centrally located areas. The fact that in less favoured regions wages are low does not compensate the expectation for higher productivity, as production output either stagnates or decreases. Less favoured regions also lack the required infrastructure which will serve industrial development and, as a consequence, competitiveness is low. Furthermore, with the completion of the internal market, less favoured regions are also challenged to reach the average European performance level, when standards of quality and efficiency in traditional labour intensive industries are evolving rapidly.

Industrial policies based on traditional forms of financial assistance to less favoured regions in the European Union can only achieve a temporary balance between them and the fully

27. See J.M. Fernadez Martin and O. Stehmann, 'Product Market Integration versus Regional Cohesion in the Community', *op. cit.* n.15 above.

developed, industrially intense regions. Such a balance will inevitably have suboptimal effects, as neither production nor productivity is expected to increase. State aids do not contribute to industrial restructuring and adjustment, unless there is provision for spatial distribution of economic activities.

Industrial policies through public procurement can also be implemented with reference to defence industries, particularly for procurement of military equipment. The procurement directives cover equipment of dual-use purchased by the armed forces, but explicitly exlude from the ambit military equipment. It should be also mentioned here that every member state in the European Union pursues its own military procurement policy by virtue of Article 223.

In the light of the Maastricht Treaty on European Union, it would appear necessary that the creation of a framework should be established within which a common European defence policy may be pursued, and that defence contracts and procurement of military equipment by member states should be harmonized, to the extent that a centralized mechanism regulating them should take over independent national military procurement practices.[28]

Attemps have been made to liberalize, to a limited extent, the procurement of military equipment at European level under the auspices of European Defence Equipment Market (EDEM). This initiative is a programme of gradual liberalization of defence industries in the relevant countries and has arisen through the oreration of the Independent European Programme Group, which has been a forum of industrial cooperation in defence industry matters among European NATO members.[29] The programme has envisaged, apart from collaborative research and development in defence technology, the introduction of a competitive regime in defence procurement and a modest degree of transparency,[30] subject to the Draconian primary Treaty provisions of Article 223. Award of defence procurement contracts under the EDEM should follow a similar rationale with civilian procurement, particularly in

28. A. Cox, 'The Future of European Defence Policy: the Case for a Centralised Procurement Agency', *Public Procurement Law Review*, 1994, Vol. 2, p.65.

29. The Independent European Programme Group has been renamed the Western European Armaments Group and its operation was transferred under the auspices of the Western European Union (WEU) in 1992.

30. Excluded from the EDEM regime are nuclear and chemical weapons, propulsion systems and warships. Exeptions from the policy commitments could also be justified on grounds of 'emergency' and 'national security'.

the introduction of award criteria based on economic and financial considerations and a minimum degree of publicity for contracts in exess of ECU 1 m.

The establishment of a common European defence policy will bring about the integration of defence industries in the European Union and this will inevitably require a change in governments' policies and practices.[31] Competitiveness, public savings considerations, value for money, transparency and non-discrimination should be the principles of the centralized mechanism regulating defence procurement in Europe. The establishment of a centralized defence agency with tasks of contractorization, facilities management and market testing are all examples of new procurement policies which give an opportunity to the defence industry for new business but at the same time create greater risks to contend with. New directions on existing policies such as risk management, contracting for reliability and cost all represent challenges for the defence industries to meet.

31. J.B. Wheaton, 'Defence Procurement and the European Community', *Public Procurement Law Review*, 1992, Vol. 1, p.432.

Concluding remarks

The efforts of European institutions to bring public procurement into conformity with the fundamental Treaty provisions prohibiting discrimination and obstacles to the free and undistorted flow of goods and services throughout the Common Market is a promising attempt for the completion of a genuine Common Market. The effectiveness of the public procurement legislation relies mainly on its decentralized application by the member states. The greater the regime of transparency they provide, the more efficient the level of competition in public markets that occurs, a fact that will result in their full integration. Empirical results reveal that contracting authorities award the vast majority of public contracts without recourse to the provisions of the relevant directives. This finding discloses the size of dimensional and sub-dimensional procurement in member states and brings into play questions concerning the utilization of sub-dimensional public procurement as a tool for policy implementation in member states. Empirical research extrapolated form the Tenders Electronic Daily and the Supplement of the *Official Journal* of the European Communities for the period 1992–95 relating to supplies and works contracts reveals that the percentages of public contracts advertised in the *Official Journal* by member states are generally very low (Belgium 7.9, Denmark 18.1, France 14.7, Germany 16.8, Greece 8.2, Ireland 11.5, Italy 50.6, Luxembourg 7.5, The Netherlands 6.5, Portugal 15.4, Spain 8.4, United Kingdom 16.4). These results justify the concerns that that the efforts of European institutions to integrate the public sector of the European Community and its member states will not change the ingrained habits of nationalistic procurement overnight.

Although it is relatively early to appraise in a general and conclusive way the impact of public procurement legislation on the process of the integration of public sector in Europe, bearing in mind that public procurement legisaltion is ineffective in some member states (the utilities directive has to be implemented by Greece and Portugal not later than 1 January, 1998), it would be useful to suggest the thorough examination of two indicators which may help us in understanding the process of public sector integration from a critical perspective, as well as to assess its progress. These indicators monitor the performance of the relevant players in the public markets and measure a number of external factors that have significant importance in shaping the post-internal market environment in relation to public procurement. The first indicator should examine the cross-border penetration of public procurement markets, which could reveal the degree of openness of the public sector in the member states and expose possible remaining patterns of protectionism in certain strategic industries, whereas the second indicator should measure any savings achieved by the public sector attributable to the enactment and implementation of the public procurement legislation, after taking into account the costs borne by national administrations for the transposition of the directives into domestic legal systems and the costs borne by the industry in adopting its selling behaviour to comply with the newly enacted regime.

European institutions have undertaken a major task in order to achieve the envisaged competitive regime in public markets and the role of the European Court of Justice and of national courts with respect to the interpretation, correct application and award of compensation to aggrieved parties will be of vital importance.

Bibliography

Advisory Committee for the Opening up of Public Procurement, *Policy Guidlines on the Obligation to refer to European Standards*, CCO/91/67 final.

Advisory Committee for the Opening up of Public Procurement, *Standards for Procurement*, CCO/92/02

P. Armin-Trepte, *Public procurement in the EC*, CCH Europe, 1993.

S. Arrowsmith, 'The Legality of Secondary Procurement Policies under the Treaty of Rome and the Works Directive', *Public Procurement Law Review*, 1992, Vol. 1.

S. Arrowsmith, 'Public Procurement as an Instrument Policy and the Impact of Market Liberalisation', *The Law Quarterly Review*, 1995, Vol. 11, p. 235.

P.J. Birkinshaw, 'Corporatism and Accountability' in *Corporatism and the Corporate State*, eds N. O'Sullivan and A. Cox, Edward Elgar, 1988.

P.J. Birkinshaw and C. Bovis, *Public Procurement: Legislation and Commentary*, Butterworths European Law Service, 1992.

C. Bovis, *Public Procurement and Small and Medium Sized Enterprises in the United Kingdom and the Republic of Ireland*, ACCA, Research Paper 17, 1996.

J. Carr, *New Roads to Equality: Contract Compliance for the United Kingdom*, Fabian Society, No. 517.

Cechinni Report *1992 The European Challenge*, Aldershot: Wildwood House, 1988.

Commission of the European Communities, *SMEs Participation in Public Procurement in the European Community* (SEC(92) 722).

Commission of the European Communities, *Action Programme for SMEs* (COM(86) 445).

Commission of the European Communities, *Public Procurement: Regional and Social Aspects* (COM(89) 400).

Commission of the European Communities, *Promoting SME Participation in the Community* (COM(90) 166).

Commission of the European Communities, *White Paper for the Completion of the Internal Market*, (COM) 85 310 fin., 1985.

Commission of the European Communities, *SME TASK FORCE: SMEs and Public Procurement*, Brussels 1988.

Commission of the European Communities, *The Cost of Non-Europe, Basic Findings,* Vol. 5, Part A; The Cost of Non-Europe in Public Sector Procurement Luxembourg: Official Publications of the European Communities, 1988.

Commission of the European Communities, *Pan European Forum on Sub-Contracting in the Community*, Brussels, 1993.

Commission of the European Communities, *Statistical Performance for Keeping watch over public procurement*, 1992.

Commission of the European Communities, *The Use of Negotiated Procedures as a Non-Tariff Barrier in Public Procurement*, Brussels, 1995.

A. Cox, *Public Procurement in the European Community: The single market rules and the enforcement regime after 1992*, Erlsgate Press, 1993.

A. Cox, 'The Future of European Defence Policy: the Case for a Centralised Procurement Agency', *Public Procurement Law Review*, 1994, Vol. 2.

T. Daintith, 'Regulation by Contract: the new prerogative', CLP, 1979, Vol. 32.

T. Daintith 'The Executive Power Today: Bargaining and Economic Control in *The Changing Constitution*, eds J. Jowell and D. Oliver, OUP, 1985, London: HMSO. The Central Statistical Office, *United Kingdom National Accounts*.

European Commission Recommendation (91/561/EEC) of October 24, 1991, on the standardisation of notices of public contracts [1991] OJ 217.

European Commission Staff Working Paper on the problem of the time taken to make payments in commercial transactions (SEC(92) (214)).

J.M Fernadez Martin and O. Stehmann, 'Product Market Integration versus Regional Cohesion in the Community, *European Law Review*, 1991, Vol. 16.

14th FIDE Congress on Application in the Member States of the Directives on Public Procurement, Madrid 1990.

de Graaf 'The political agreement on a common position concerning the utilities services Directive', *Public Procurement Law Review*, 1992.

L. Gormley, 'Some Reflections on Public Procurement in the EEC', (Nov. 1990) *European Business Law Review*.

I. Harden, 'Defining the range of application of the public sector procurement Directives in the United Kingdom', *Public Procurement Law Review* 1992, Vol. 1.

ILEA Contract Compliance Equal Opportunities Unit, *Contract Compliance: a Brief History*, 1990.

Institute of Personnel Management, *Contract Compliance: The United Kingdom Experience*, 1987.

The Internal Market after 1992 – Meeting the Challenge. Report to the E.C. Commission by the High Level Group on the Internal Market (Sutherland), November 1992.

D. Mardas, 'Sub-contracting, Small and Medium Sized Enterprises (SMEs) and Public Procurement in the European Community', *Public Procurement Law Review*, 1994, Vol. 3.

P.E. Morris, 'Legal Regulation of Contract Compliance: an Anglo-American Comparison', *Anglo-American Law Review*, 1990, Vol. 19.

G. O'Brien, 'Public Procurement and the Small or Medium Sized Enterprise', *Public Procurement Law Review*, 1993, Vol. 2.

N. O'Loan, Implementation of Directive 90/531 and Directive 92/50 in the United Kingdom, *Public Procurement Law Review*, 1993, p. 29.

Kapteyn and Verloren van Themaat, *Introduction to the Law of the European Communities*, 3rd edn Deventer: Kluwer, 1989.

F. Weiss, 'The law of Public Procurement in EFTA and the EEC; the legal framework and its implementation', *Yearbook of European Law*, 1987.

F. Weiss, 'Public Procurement in the EEC-Public Supply Contracts', (1988) *European Law Review*.

J.B. Wheaton, 'Defence Procurement and the European Community,' *Public Procurement Law Review*, 1992, Vol. 1.

H. Winter, 'Direct applicability and direct effective of EC Law', [1972] 9 CMLRev 425.

Further reading

A number of books on public procurement have been published in English. The reader is referred to the following list of authors for further reading and references.

P. Armin-Trepte, *Public Procurement in the EC*, CCH Europe, 1993.

S. Arrowsmith, *The Law of Public and Utilities Procurement*, Sweet & Maxwell, 1996

A. Cox, *Public Procurement in the European Community: The single market rules and the enforcement regime after 1992*, Earlsgate Press, 1993.

P. Lee, *Public Procurement, Current EC Legal Developments*, Butterworths, 1992

Public Procurement: Legislation and Commentary, Butterworths European Law Service, 1992.

F. Weiss, *Public Procurement in European Law*, Athlone Publishers, 1992

For the most up-to-date reference on current legal and other developments relating to public procurement law and policy, *Public Procurement Law Review*, a journal published by Sweet & Maxwell is the best source. For a comprehensive reference on the current bibliography on public procurement, the reader is referred to *Bibliographie des Marchés Publics*, Commission of the European Communities, CCO/93/49, 1993

Useful Contacts

Commission of the European Communities, Directorate General XV, Internal Market and Industrial Affairs, Units A and B, Avenue de Cortenberg 100, B-1040, Brussels, Belgium, tel: 32 2 295 0127, fax: 32 2 296 58 26

HM Treasury, Central Unit on Procurement, Allington Towers, 19 Allington Street, London SW1E 5EB, tel: 0171 270 1628

Domestic statistical information referred to in this book was supplied by the relevant countries' national statistical departments, ministries of finance and treasuries.

Index